What Did Jesus DO All Day?

FELICIA SILCOX

What Did Jesus DO All Day?

Discovering the Teen Jesus

Morehouse Publishing
NEW YORK · HARRISBURG · DENVER

Morehouse Publishing, 4775 Linglestown Road, Harrisburg, PA 17112

Morehouse Publishing, 445 Fifth Avenue, New York, NY 10016

Morehouse Publishing is an imprint of Church Publishing Incorporated.
www.churchpublishing.org

Cover design by Laurie Klein Westhafer
Typeset by Beth Oberholtzer

Library of Congress Cataloging-in-Publication Data

Silcox, Felicia.
    What did Jesus do all day? : discovering the teen Jesus / Felicia Silcox.
        pages   cm
    Includes bibliographical references.
    ISBN 978-0-8192-2793-5 (pbk.) — ISBN 978-0-8192-2794-2 (ebook)
1. Jesus Christ—Childhood.   I. Title.
BT320.S55   2013
232.9—dc23
                                                                    2012050162

Printed in the United States of America

In memory of my parents and grandparents,
in gratitude for my children and grandchildren.

Contents

Acknowledgments

Words cannot express my deep admiration and heartfelt thanks to Joan Castagnone. More than a superb editor, Joan is an amazing person, who met our final production schedule while helping her neighbors in need after Hurricane Sandy hit. Her kindness, patience, tolerance, vision, open-mindedness, encouragement, humor, and impeccable eye brought a labor of love to fruition.

Special thanks to Laurie Westhafer for her cover design, Ryan Masteller for making all the pieces fit, and everyone at Morehouse Publishing.

Two biblical scholars graciously gave time and indispensable help to this project: David Bivin, whose work in Judaic-Christian studies at Jerusalem Perspective brings new light to Jesus' words, and Todd Bolen, who provided outstanding photos of Holy Land sites.

Grateful recognition also goes to Sue Bradford Edwards for bringing focus to the original idea, Jeni Bell Williams for being the best critique partner and true friend anyone could wish for, Marisa Reilly for her enduring encouragement and thoughtful reading of the manuscript, and Lucy and George Fendler for their tireless help with the book's website.

There are countless others, family and friends, who opened my mind to new possibilities and offered sound advice and boundless inspiration, especially Jeanette Truskot, Marian May, Kate Miller, Kriss Costa, Joyce Moody, Linda Legari, Mary Lou Carney, Mary Ann Fischer, and Chorbishop Seely Beggiani. Thank you all.

Finally, I owe an eternal debt of gratitude to my husband, Don, who encouraged me to write so many years ago, and has remained my constant support and loving companion.

May this book be a blessing to all who read it.

Introduction

What Did Jesus DO All Day? is intended to be a bridge to the world teen Jesus knew, the Holy Land in the first century. Though dominated by the Roman Empire and steeped in Torah, Jesus' world feels eerily familiar the more we learn about it. In a way, it's our world, too. Though its cultural setting and languages are vastly different, we find that human needs, as well as human nature, never change.

This book features a time line, glossary, and bibliography. Each chapter has Scripture references (New Revised Standard Version) and questions for discussion. Words, names, and terms listed in the glossary are bolded in the first usage in the book. Also included are photos of several archaeological discoveries that allow us to see—even touch—fragments of the world where Jesus lived and preached.

For more about the scholars quoted in this book, please refer to the selected bibliography. Also, visit the book's website at http://www.whatdidjesusdoallday.com. From the home page, click any link for more information: Jesus' World; Biblical Archaeology; Dead Sea Scrolls; Ancient Writings; Jewish Culture; Holy Land News; Photos, Blogs, and Other Resources; Book Updates, including suggested activities, article sources, and more websites for key word searches; and Contact Information.

We hope that discovering Jesus' world will flesh out your image of teen Jesus and bring to life who he was—a brilliant, complex Jewish youth who lived an ordinary life that hid an extraordinary reality: his kingdom was not from this world (John 18:36).

ONE

Ruins, Caves, and Ancient Scrolls: The Story Begins

For everything there is a season, and a time for every matter under heaven.
—Ecclesiastes 3:1

Tawny bluffs tower above the Judean desert, a barren wilderness blocked by mountains from much of the rain that blows inland from the Mediterranean Sea. Streaked by erosion and pitted with caves, these steep limestone cliffs overlook the northwest shore of the **Dead Sea**—and the ruins of an ancient Jewish settlement called Qumran.

In 1947, Arab Bedouin shepherds tossed a stone into one of the caves, hoping to scare out a lost sheep. The sound of breaking pottery drew them inside, where they found manuscripts, some wrapped in linen cloth that was green with age, stuffed inside tall clay storage jars. The young nomads had accidentally found the first Dead Sea Scrolls, possibly the most important archaeological discovery of the twentieth century. The Scrolls' ancient age, and what they revealed, linked them to the world Jesus knew.

For nine years, Bedouin tribesmen, along with teams of archaeologists, combed eleven caves near Qumran in search of more scrolls. Most of the scroll fragments they found, buried under rocky debris and bat droppings, were written on parchment (softened animal

The rugged Judean wilderness and Dead Sea, where a piece of Jesus' world came to light.

skins, hand-sewn together with linen thread). A few were written on sheets of papyrus (paper made from strips of the reedlike plant's stems). One scroll was made of copper. Brittle with age and gnawed by rodents, only about ten scrolls were intact.

What Were the Dead Sea Scrolls?

For years, scholars tried to match and piece together thousands of fragments into more than 900 documents. Of these, more than 200 represented nearly every one of the twenty-four canonical books of Hebrew Scripture. A few biblical books we know today, like Esther, were missing. But in Jesus' day, the Hebrew Bible did not yet have a fixed canon, or an authoritative list of sacred books.

Some of the Dead Sea Scrolls contain biblical texts that had never been seen. Others contain duplicate copies of the same book—for example, there are twenty-two copies of Isaiah, which is often quoted in the New Testament. Different versions of some texts also surfaced. Best preserved in the dry desert and the dark jars was the 23½-foot-long Isaiah Scroll, the only book found in its entirety.

What makes the Dead Sea Scrolls priceless? We now have access to Scripture texts so old they might be written in their original Hebrew form, though we can't know for sure. But we do know that some of them are written in Aramaic, which is most likely the language that Jesus spoke. This knowledge allows comparison of these older writings with translations that were written much later. It's very possible the Dead Sea Scrolls preserve the same words Jesus learned by heart when he studied—and lived by—the Hebrew Bible.

Other Writings at Qumran

Archaeologists also found fragments of nonbiblical manuscripts—the writings of people who had inhabited the caves before, during, and after Jesus' lifetime. Their works included a Community Rule scroll and a War scroll, in which "Children of Light" battle "Children of Darkness." Who were they and what were they doing at Qumran?

Though only a day's journey from Jerusalem, Qumran was located in the harsh Judean desert. Evidence shows several different groups retreated there, beginning around 150 BC. By 31 BC, the original structures had been enlarged and the site expanded into a community center for 150 to 200 people. It is generally assumed that a religious group called **Essenes** occupied the settlement around Jesus' time.

Who Were the Essenes and How Did They Live?

Josephus, a Jewish historian who lived around 37 to 100 AD, wrote that the deeply religious Essenes made up the third-largest group within Judaism, after **Sadducees** and **Pharisees**. Devoted to the Law, they rejected the other groups' authority, priesthood, and worship—

and parted ways. The Essenes, who thought the high **priests** were corrupt, likely sprang from disillusioned Temple priests during the time of the **Hasmonean** royal family (150 BC–37 BC), when each succeeding king also acted as high priest.

According to Josephus, Essenes brought no wives or slaves to the village communities or outlying settlements. They assembled daily for prayer, supported themselves by working at whatever trade or chores an overseer/director decided, enforced a three-year probation period for newcomers, observed strict ritual purity, which entailed frequent and total immersion in a ritual bath or *mikveh*, prepared for the End Days, wore their sandals to shreds, and dressed in white robes cinched with a girdle, or belt.

The Essenes shared everything they had equally, lived by and large celibately, and obeyed their overseer in most things. There were some exceptions to the rule. For example, they were free to assist the needy without asking his permission. This austere lifestyle parallels the poverty, chastity, and obedience practiced in Christian monasteries hundreds of years later.

The Qumran Community's Lifestyle/ Qumran's Destruction

The residents of Qumran rose before dawn every day, prayed, observed periods of silence, and bathed in cold water. Their emphasis on frequent immersion and the Last Judgment leads many to think John the Baptist—who baptized his followers in the **Jordan River** nearby—followed their teachings.

Qumran's well-preserved ruins indicate that the inhabitants ate meals together in a long dining hall, where archaeologists discovered hundreds of plates, bowls, and cups. They might have copied manuscripts in a room where three ancient objects—believed by many to be inkwells—were found. Oil lamps scattered in a possible study room, adjacent to what could have been a scroll library, hint that the community studied there a third of the night, as their book of rules required.

Archaeological finds reveal the Qumran community's lifestyle: they ate, studied, and worked together inside the complex, but likely lived in nearby shelters or in caves in the limestone cliffs, about a mile away. Natural erosion had formed most of the caves. Others had been dug out of the soft, crumbly rock by hand. Those shelters had multiple openings that let in a crosscurrent of breezes, natural air conditioning in the desert heat.

There is evidence of a fire at Qumran around 37 BC and destruction from the severe earthquake of 31 BC, which was reported by Josephus. Briefly abandoned, the site was later rebuilt. But in 68 AD, the Romans leveled the complex on their way to destroy Jerusalem and end the **First Great Jewish Revolt** (66–70 AD). The caves were also occupied—and invaded—during the **Second Great Jewish Revolt** (132–135 AD).

The Dead Sea Scrolls found so far—dated from the third century BC to the first century AD and written in Hebrew, Aramaic, and Greek—raise many questions. For example, who wrote them, who hid them, and when? Did they all originate at Qumran? Or, is it possible some biblical scrolls came from the **Second Temple**, carried by those who escaped the Romans' plunder of Jerusalem? For more information about this time, we turn to a first-century eyewitness named Josephus.

Some Dead Sea Scrolls and **Torah** scrolls are so fragile that they crumble when handled. These haven't yet been read, so scientists hope to use scans to "unroll" them. Images of other rolled documents (more recent, though still ancient) have been taken at different angles using "super X-rays"—generated by synchrotron light beams that are millions of times brighter than our sun. After analyzing the scan results, in the form of computerized data, experts can "read" the rolled-up texts in their original form. Read about Britain's Diamond synchrotron and see an animation at http://news.bbc.co.uk/2/hi/science/nature/6991893.stm.

The Jewish Historian Josephus

Josephus Flavius was Jewish, a well-educated son of a noblewoman and a priest. As a teen, he studied with a desert hermit before becoming a Pharisee. When unrest from Roman cruelty, as well as Jewish rebels fighting one another for control, exploded in the First Great Revolt, Josephus commanded rebel troops in Galilee. In 66 AD the Roman army, commanded by General Vespasian, besieged his stronghold town of Jotapata, about eleven miles north of Nazareth. Most of the defenders committed suicide, rather than face defeat. Josephus surrendered—and his fellow Jews saw him as a cowardly traitor.

While in chains, Josephus predicted Vespasian would become Emperor, which he did in 69 AD. When he returned to Rome to rule, Vespasian left his son Titus in charge of the war and made Josephus an interpreter and go-between with the Jewish rebels. Thus, Josephus witnessed firsthand Jerusalem's destruction in 70 AD and the rebels' fall at Masada in 73 AD. His writings, composed later in Rome, include a history of the Jewish people. He adopted the surname "Flavius," Vespasian's family name.

Today, we read Josephus' works with caution. He contradicted himself at times, wrote from his aristocratic bias, and exaggerated historical facts—although that was the common epic writing style of his day. Though Jewish, he served pagan Rome and always portrayed his protectors in a good light. But what Josephus said about Jerusalem's destruction might explain why many scrolls ended up in the desert around the Dead Sea.

The Siege of Jerusalem

In 70 AD, General Titus led the Roman army against Jerusalem. He surrounded the city, cutting off food and water. The siege lasted from April to September, hot and dry months. Inside the city's protective walls, disease and famine followed. Some Jews tried to flee the coming destruction; those caught outside the city walls were crucified.

Other residents hid in "caverns/mines" or "underground passages," where many died of hunger. Once the Romans breached the walls and entered Jerusalem, Josephus wrote, they massacred thousands—both above ground and below. But strong young men were not killed; rather, they were captured to be slaves or gladiators. But Josephus' words, "underground passages," were puzzling. What exactly did he mean?

In 2007, workers in Jerusalem uncovered part of the city's ancient "main drainage channel" or sewer system, along with pots, oil lamps, coins, a key, and a Roman sword and sheath—all from the time of the siege. Above this vast underground tunnel, a stone-paved street led upward, in broad steps, from the **Pool of Siloam** to the Temple's western wall. The tunnel's walls, made of huge stone blocks, stretched as much as ten feet high in some places. It's likely some survivors used the sewer system to escape—before Roman soldiers hacked holes into the street above and found their hideout.

Jerusalem's drainage channel likely emptied into the nearby Kidron River, which flows about thirteen miles east to the Dead Sea. Surrounded by gorges, the Kidron *wadi* (riverbed) was bone dry during the summer. The terrified escapees, on foot and carrying their belongings, probably followed the dusty *wadi* as it descended from Jerusalem's heights. About halfway to the Dead Sea, the riverbed branched off into a second *wadi* that led to Qumran—and the safety of its caves.

Josephus said Titus took back to Rome the Temple's golden seven-branched candlestick, a gold table, and a copy of the Law. But Baruch Safrai, who helped in the original search of Qumran's caves, thinks Jerusalem's refugees rescued many Scripture scrolls and possibly other Temple treasures. In *The Dead Sea Scrolls*, he writes that these might still lie buried at Qumran or elsewhere. In fact, the 7½-foot-long Copper Scroll, inscribed on metal sheets, lists "sixty-four hiding places of huge amounts of gold and silver."

The Dead Sea Scrolls and Christianity

The Dead Sea Scrolls reveal a valuable tie to Jesus' life—Judaism and Christianity were built on the same foundation. One scroll, the

Damascus Document, refers to members of the Qumran community being true to a **New Covenant**, rather than the people's **Old Covenant**, made with God on Mount Sinai. Members renewed their Covenant every year, during the Jewish feast of **Pentecost**.

Many websites are now dedicated to the Dead Sea Scrolls and the Qumran community. A key word search will turn up a lot of information.

One of the scrolls contains a prayer members recited during ritual immersion, which connects repentance with spiritual cleansing. John the Baptist called people to repent before he baptized them by immersion in the Jordan River.

Yet another scroll refers to the "Son of God" and "son of the Most High," titles also found in the Hebrew Bible. This scroll shows that Jews, even before Jesus' time, were using those words to refer to a future **Messiah**. Here is yet another way the Dead Sea Scrolls reveal the common origin of Judaism and Christianity.

Jesus lived in the Holy Land when many of the scrolls found at Qumran were still being copied by hand. What was life like back

Photo Credit: Todd Bolen/BiblePlaces.com

Dead Sea Scroll fragment, one of thousands found in Qumran.

then? With help from historians and archaeologists, we can go back in time and find out.

Questions for Discussion

1. If you were to visit Qumran (or any other biblical site) someday and take part in a dig, what do you think you would look for? What would be the most exciting discovery you could make?

2. What did you find to be the most interesting or surprising revelation in the Dead Sea Scrolls?

TWO

The Tale a Dead Man Told

But now if any one hath a mind to come over to their [Essene] sect . . . they give him also a small hatchet, and the fore-mentioned girdle, and the white garment.

—Josephus, *The Wars of the Jews*

By 1953, six years had passed since the first Dead Sea Scrolls were discovered in the Judean Desert. There, Baruch Safrai—a young member of an archaeology team—dangled along a steep cliff face on a sixty-foot rope ladder, secured from above. At last, he reached the narrow opening of a cave—later named the "Cave of Letters," because it held a cache of rare personal documents—and pulled himself through it.

At one time, the vast cave had collapsed. Standing inside one of its three exposed chambers, Safrai's eyes widened. A cascade of boulders, twenty feet high and covered with bat dung, stretched toward the thirty-foot-tall ceiling. Clouds of acrid dust choked him as he shifted enough rocks to open a narrow gap in the rubble.

Clutching his flashlight, Safai slipped through the tight space and inched his way downward into the darkness far below. Suddenly he froze. His light beam darted back and forth across a sprawled skeleton, pinned under heavy boulders. Draping the bones was a white robe, tied with a rope belt that was knotted in front.

After alerting his team's leader to his find, Safari returned to
squeeze back in among the sharp rocks and drop down again to the
skeleton. When he tried to remove what he could, the upper halves
of the robe and belt came off in his hands—the undersides had rotted away. But those fragments offered exciting clues to the skeleton's
identity. Could he have been an Essene?

Safrai's team knew the Essenes always wore cinched, white robes
and guessed the dead man had belonged to that sect. Josephus had

Aerial view of Qumran's excavations and cliffs, with wadi (riverbed) below.

reported that a major earthquake struck the region in 31 BC. If the man had died in that earthquake, he'd have lived close to Jesus' time. But was that when the man died? The lead archaeologist placed the robe and belt in a padded cardboard box, to be carried back to Jerusalem. More work lay ahead.

When archaeologists dated other finds from the same cave, they discovered it had been occupied during the First and the Second Great Jewish Revolts, both of which occurred *after* Jesus' lifetime. However, they found their evidence for this conclusion on top of the collapsed cave roof, *not* from the lower level where Safrai found the skeleton.

Sad to say, the box containing the robe and belt was "lost, stolen, or forgotten on the way," wrote Safrai in *The Dead Sea Scrolls,* so its contents were never dated. Excavation of the cave's depths, where the man's bones still lie buried under tons of rubble, might reveal when he had lived there. At the time of the discovery, archaeologists lacked the equipment needed to dig down so far. Today, researchers have the high-tech equipment capable of reaching that remote area, but they lack funding to support such a challenging project.

What the Gospels Say—and Don't Say

Qumran was occupied during the lifetimes of Jesus and his cousin, John the Baptist, who both sought God in the desert wilderness. So, in Qumran's caves, archaeologists touched the world Jesus knew, the world of the Gospels. The Gospels chronicle major events in his life: his birth, his family fleeing King Herod's murderous rage and becoming homeless immigrants in Egypt, their return to Nazareth after Herod's death, Jesus' Passover pilgrimage to the Temple at age twelve, his teachings and miracles as a teacher, his crucifixion, and his resurrection from the dead.

But the Gospel writers left out details about Jesus' everyday life. Why? Because Jesus' world was their world, too. It was totally familiar to them and to their first-century audience. For them, its customs and lifestyle needed no explanation. Think of it this way. You don't stop and explain to your friends how a cell phone works or how to play a computer game. It's understood. Similarly, the Gospel writers felt no need to chronicle the mundane details of their time.

What about us, twenty-one centuries later? Though we can't know Jesus' world with certainty, there *are* ways we can see into it—and find surprising similarities, like homework, housework, community worship, relaxing on holidays, celebrating weddings, mourning at funerals, and dealing with government-related problems.

Reconstructing the Past

Earthquakes, erosion, and war have all changed the landscape of the Holy Land. Much of the physical evidence from Jesus' time, including entire towns, lies deep within the earth. That's why archaeology matters. It uncovers the past and tells the story of ancient people. With great patience, archaeologists use tools that include brushes, tweezers, and spoons to "read" the part of the story each new site (dig) tells.

Today, occupation of the territory once known as the Holy Land is hotly disputed. Archaeologists are caught in the political crossfire of Jews, Muslims, and Christians who live there, as no group wants access to its holy sites disturbed. Fortunately, scholars explored the Holy Land during quieter times (the 1800s to mid-1900s) and produced detailed maps, drawings, and writings that are now indispensable. Jerusalem landmarks bear their names: Robinson's Arch, Warren's Gate, Wilson's Arch, and Barclay's Gate.

Archaeologists mark off sites, excavate, and gather soil samples for chemical analysis. They sift multiple layers of earth; each represents a period in time and yields evidence of past activity. For example, "burn layers" are black. Diggers also look for artifacts—ancient manmade objects—embedded in the layers: pottery, scrolls, seals, coins, building remains, stone jugs, jars, oil lamps, inscriptions, tools, mosaic tiles, arrowheads, spears, and bone boxes. Jewish markers include **ritual baths** or the absence of pork bones in garbage heaps. Contents of ancient toilets reveal what people ate—or hid. Found buried for safekeeping inside the Cave of Letters' toilet were nineteen bronze vessels, including incense shovels, wine decanters, and a shallow bowl. All finds are carefully cleaned, dated, and preserved.

Radiocarbon dating, used on bone and wood, won't work with pottery, brick, or tile since clay doesn't contain carbon. However, it is possible to date earthenware samples by measuring changes in mass due to moisture loss after kiln firing. But a well-trained eye can spot tiny differences between pottery made during the Hasmonean Dynasty (150–37 BC) and pots made during the next reign, that of **King Herod the Great** and his descendants (37 BC–70 AD). Chemical analysis of clay reveals a potter's general region. Other technologies—like aerial photography, GPS, GIS, GPR, and OSL—help archaeologists, too.

Global Positioning Systems (GPS) record the coordinates of a dig's location. Geographic Information Systems (GIS) record where each artifact is found. Satellite images and topographic maps record surface features, while Ground Penetrating Radar (GPR) shows ruins below the terrain. Using these data, it is possible to create a 3-D virtual model of an ancient archaeological site. Optically Stimulated Luminescence (OSL), used to date soil, helps archaeologists reconstruct periods of occupation.

Digging is a destructive process. However, archaeologists can now "see" 3-D images of buried artifacts without the drawbacks of excavation. British archaeologists and engineers took thousands of X-ray images of a hoard of Roman gold coins, concreted inside an ancient urn. See a video animation of their results at http://www.biblicalarchaeology.org.

Archaeologists aren't alone in their search for the biblical past. Historians, forensic scientists, experts in Mediterranean culture, and biblical scholars (both Christian and Jewish) are also working to reconstruct Jesus' world. But there are ways to learn from the way people live today. Middle Easterners greatly value tradition. Therefore much of their ancient culture—food, dress, and customs related to family and honor—remains similar to what it was in biblical times.

Thanks to these studies, today's researchers extrapolate valuable information about the world in which Jesus grew up. They continue to discover, piece together, and revise (as new evidence emerges) details about the lifestyle of ordinary Jewish families in the first-century Holy Land—especially the years between Herod the Great's rule and the Romans' destruction of Jerusalem (40 BC–70 AD), that part of the **Second Temple Period** that includes Jesus' lifetime. Now, twenty-one centuries later, we can come close to knowing what teen Jesus did all day.

What If You Were There?

So, what *was* life like back then? If you were a Jewish teen in Jesus' time, your life would revolve around family honor and obeying Torah, the Law of Moses, which you'd learn and study with your family (at home) and other villagers (in the **synagogue**). You'd hear **rabbis** or Pharisees teach right behavior according to their interpretations of Scripture. "Rabbi" means "my master" in Hebrew and was a respectful form of address, used for a sage or learned teacher. The rabbis' interpretations often differed and were argued in public.

How would you know what was going on the world? Women and girls chatted at **Nazareth**'s village well every morning after they moved the flat rock that covered its top, drew household water with a clay pot attached to a rope, and filled nearby animal troughs. Men met in public marketplaces, where they exchanged news and gossip.

What about school? It is believed that Jewish boys ages five to thirteen attended the village synagogue every day for Bible study. No books—the printing press was centuries in the future. Boys, you'd repeat and memorize every word your teacher taught. Girls, you weren't allowed to attend school, so you'd help with chores at home all day.

The Temple was in Jerusalem, sixty-five miles south of your village of Nazareth, in the northern region of **Galilee**. How would you go to church on Sunday? You wouldn't. You'd observe the weekly **Sabbath** at home with your family.

Sheep drinking at well, where women and girls mingled—and checked out village boys.

Every spring, you might walk to Jerusalem for the great feast of **Passover** and join other Jewish families in worship. There, the Temple high priest (one of the Sadducees) would offer the sacrificial liturgy. Maybe your family would decide to take a shortcut through the country's middle region, **Samaria**. But Samaritans offered no hospitality to Jews passing through their land; worse, animosity flared on both sides. Taking a longer, but safer, route would extend your travel time—already four to seven days one way, depending on how many miles your family could cover in a day.

There were no picnic coolers, restaurants, or fast-food places. How would you eat while traveling? You'd pack portable meals: toasted grain, dried fruit, pressed cakes of figs or raisins with nuts and seeds, cheese, olives, and a goatskin filled with water or watered-down wine. You'd let your pack animal drink from your cupped hands and replenish water at a well or oasis. Every rest stop made

Photo Credit: Todd Bolen/BiblePlaces.com

The Tale a Dead Man Told

17

your journey longer. At night, you'd need to find a shelter, safe from roaming bands of robbers. But no inconvenience would bother you. Seeing Jerusalem's splendors was worth the trouble of getting there!

And there were no toothbrushes. How would you keep your breath fresh? You'd chew licorice-tasting anise seeds, mint leaves, or the gummy resin of the terebinth tree, which is in the cashew family. Craving sweets? You'd search among rocky crevices for wild honeycomb. If chewing it made your cavities hurt, garlic and saltwater or terebinth gum might ease the pain. One ancient skull, dated 200 BC, had a bronze wire filling, but most people's decayed teeth rotted away—or someone pulled them. Forget about pizza. Like chocolate, tomatoes hadn't yet arrived in the Holy Land.

Body-conscious pagans "worked out" to keep fit. But you'd build muscles by doing hard physical work to help your family survive. You'd grow up fast. By the time you were twelve, your parents would expect you to accept responsibility for family, village, and tribal honor—or else. "The rod . . . gives wisdom" (Proverbs 29:15). No crying or complaining allowed.

To buy new sandals or a belt, you'd go to an open-air market or bazaar in the nearest big town and wander down narrow streets lined with vendors' stalls and small shops. You'd argue loudly over the price. Maybe you'd offer the seller a service you could provide, or something you made or grew, in exchange for what you wanted.

If your village didn't grow its own grain or nuts, shopping was trickier. There were no scales or scientific standards of measurement in the markets. You'd watch the vendor like a hawk while he scooped out your agreed-upon portion.

As a young Jew in a warm dry climate, you'd bathe frequently and apply olive oil, perhaps scented with rose petals or other flowers, to soften your skin. Olive oil massaged into your hair helped protect you against sunburn—and head lice, which were common. The Bible also mentions "perfumers," who sold heavenly smelling, but very expensive fragrances and exotic ointments like balsam, myrrh, cassia, and nard.

Girls and boys didn't attend school together—and, once they turned thirteen and became proper Jewish "men," boys didn't speak to women in public. So how would you get to know each other? Boys, when you left home very early in the morning for school or work, you'd eye a pretty girl as she waited her turn to draw water at the village well. Hopefully, she'd eye you back. Weddings and holidays would give you a chance to mingle. If you decided she was the special one, you'd hint for your parents to arrange your marriage.

You'd probably play a reed flute and maybe a stringed instrument, like a lyre. Flute music was heard everywhere, especially at weddings and funerals. You'd also shake a tambourine (rhythm ruled in Jewish music!) and join in group singing at celebrations. During Temple worship, the choir and congregation sang psalms and hymns in one mighty voice, but without any harmony—something like medieval chant.

No curfew for you, but the whims of your king, **Herod Antipas**— and the no-nonsense Roman conquerors who made their presence known—determined the limits of your freedom. The Romans were BIG on not disturbing the peace and publicly crucified rebels and protesters. The **Sanhedrin** (High Council/Supreme Court) could also condemn you to death for a serious violation of Moses' Law, the religious law of the land.

There were no hospitals or emergency clinics, so what would you do if you suffered a bad cut or burn? You'd apply olive oil to soothe the pain, as well as wine, honey, cumin (which also helped stop bleeding), and/or fig sap. All contained natural antibiotics to prevent or fight infection in wounds. You'd treat a sore throat or an eye disease with bee honey.

You'd totally stress over any seemingly harmless rash, blotch, or pimple. If your skin ailment didn't resolve quickly, a Temple priest would have to examine it and might mistake it for leprosy. People feared lepers, whose disfiguring sores ritually contaminated everyone and everything they touched. You'd have to live alone outside your village and cry "Unclean!" when anyone came near—until your skin healed and a priest allowed you to return home. It's uncertain what biblical leprosy really was, since descriptions of it in Torah vary. Actual leprosy, or Hansen's disease, is only slightly contagious. But DNA testing confirmed the existence of Hansen's disease in a shroud and skeleton found in a first-century Jerusalem tomb.

What if you were blind, deaf, or lame—common ailments in Jesus' time—or suffered from a serious illness? People would think God was punishing you. Your parents might take you for treatment to a hot spring near the **Sea of Galilee** or the Dead Sea. Maybe they'd seek out a holy man to free you from a demon, or ask the village doctor for a plant remedy. In the end, you might not survive. In *The Cultural Dictionary of the Bible*, John Pilch writes that six out of ten children died before age sixteen.

That's just the beginning of what life was like for a teen in Jesus' world.

Questions for Discussion

1. Jesus' teen years were very different than they are today. If you could go back 2,000 years and spend a week or two in Nazareth, what do you think you'd enjoy? What do you think you would totally hate?

2. Day-to-day life changes so much over time. And don't you get tired of hearing that line, "When I was your age . . . ?" For example, your parents or grandparents might vividly remember their first cell phone, while you never knew life without one. How do you talk about things you take for granted? Imagine talking to someone your age, but who lived in 1900. How would you explain what an Xbox is and the technology that makes it possible?

3. How has an event or discovery in your life thrown light on the past? Maybe you found an old letter or photograph. Maybe someone told you a family story you'd never heard before.

THREE

Jesus' World: How It Looked and Who Shaped It

Be careful with the ruling power, for they bring no man near to them except for their own interests: they seem to be friends in time of their own advantage, and they do not stand with a man in the hour of his need.

—Mishna

The Romans called the geographical region of Jesus' homeland, Roman Judea. Jews were known as Judeans. Roman Judea was divided into three parts. The southern part, also called **Judea**, was the old Kingdom of Judah; Bethlehem and Jerusalem were located there. Samaria occupied the central region; a large cosmopolitan city there, Sebaste, had pagan residents. In the northern region of Galilee, Jesus grew up in the village of Nazareth. He taught and healed mostly in towns that circled the Sea of Galilee.

Jesus' Jewish World: How It Looked on the Outside

Jesus' homeland has a mild climate with two basic seasons: hot, dry summer days usually cooled at night by sea breezes and dew and a chilly winter with heavy rains, icy winds, and sometimes even snow. Temperatures can drop seventy degrees between noon and midnight.

At times, a *khamsin* (blistering wind) blows in from the Negev Desert, parching the earth and human skin. A cold whirlwind-making *qadim* still whips up sudden and violent storms, like the one Jesus calmed, on the Sea of Galilee.

Moving inland from the Mediterranean, the sandy coast gives way to fertile plains and rolling hills that stretch inland to the Judean Mountains. This range, sometimes called the Holy Land's backbone, extends from the Negev Desert in the south to Galilee in the north. Jerusalem sits atop its ridge. Approaching travelers in Jesus' day saw it from afar.

On their far side, the heights plunge into the deep, narrow Jordan Valley—part of the Great Rift, a trench with earthquake faults, volcanoes, and hot springs that stretches into Africa. Here lies the Jordan River where Jesus was baptized, the desert wilderness where he fasted and prayed, the Dead Sea (with the earth's saltiest water and its lowest place, at 1,300 feet below sea level), and the Sea of Galilee, which is actually a freshwater lake.

As a rabbi, Jesus was drawn to the Sea of Galilee, also called the Sea of Tiberias or Lake of Gennesaret, and known in the Hebrew Bible as the Sea of Kinnereth. The word *kinnor*, which means "harp," likely referred to the lake's shape. More than twenty species of fish live in its waters today, including sardines, tilapia or "St. Peter's fish," and catfish, which is thrown away by Jewish fishermen because they are "unclean," or not fit to eat.

Jesus' Jewish World: How It Looked on the Inside

Within Judaism, Jesus encountered many schools of religious thought, whose influence often extended into politics. Pharisees, Sadducees, **scribes**, Essenes, **Herodians**, and **Zealots** all believed in one God and Moses' Law, but had different interpretations of the Law—and followed very different lifestyles. Josephus described Essenes, but what is known about the other major Jewish sects?

Pharisees/Rabbis

Teen Jesus was studying to be a teacher or rabbi, which would have aligned him with the Pharisees. They were not priests, but lay scholars and teachers, many of them traveling rabbis, who took pride in living "pure" Judaism. Their devout behavior, learning, kindness to one another, and modest lifestyle earned the people's respect.

Pharisees commonly debated one another in public—and Jesus often disagreed with them. Yet many of his Scripture interpretations were similar to their basic teachings. Some Pharisees admired Jesus and shared his views. Nicodemus "came to Jesus by night" to learn from him (John 3:1–2). Joseph of Arimathea, a "secret" disciple, gave his tomb for Jesus' burial (John 19:38). St. Paul was likely a Pharisee.

Pharisees believed in both Oral and Written **Torah**, the Prophets' writings, repentance, free will, miracles, angels, the kingdom of heaven, the coming of the Messiah, end times, and resurrection of the dead. However, they gave Oral Torah—their interpretations of Scripture—so much authority that Jesus harshly criticized them. "You abandon the commandment of God and hold to human tradition" (Mark 7:8).

Sadducees/Priests

Sadducees belonged to the powerful priestly aristocracy that ruled the Temple and its worship liturgy. Priests descended from Levi's tribe through Aaron, brother of Moses. High priests descended from the royal Hasmonean family. Allied with Rome and opponents of the Pharisees, most Sadducees were wealthy, haughty, and strict in judgments. They accepted *only* Written Torah. Heavily influenced by Greek thinking, they didn't believe in an afterlife, angels, or resurrection. Most Jews disliked them.

The Sanhedrin/High Court

A council of seventy-one members—sages or wise men from *both* the Pharisees and the Sadducees—formed the Sanhedrin or High Court, the highest judicial authority of the Jewish people, comparable to our

Supreme Court. Its members met daily in the Temple's Chamber of Hewn Stone, where they studied Torah, passed laws, and delivered judgments on major religious and civil matters. The Sanhedrin had power to condemn to death (usually by stoning) someone found guilty of a serious offense against Jewish religious law. In cities and towns large enough to be surrounded by gated walls, respected elders sat "before the gate," where the public marketplace was located, and heard minor disputes.

Scribes

Highly educated and respected, scribes wrote and kept correspondence, hand-copied sacred writings, and recorded events. In *The Cultural World of Jesus*, John Pilch writes that they were "Scripture scholars," who specialized in Torah and its observance. Several scribes became famous doctors of the Law. Many scribes *agreed* with the Pharisees' way of thinking, especially regarding Oral Torah—but not all scribes *were* Pharisees.

Photo Credit: Todd Bolen/BiblePlaces.com

Modern Jewish scribe copying Scripture by hand, work that requires patient attention to detail.

Three brilliant first-century Pharisee scribes had a school and followers. Shammai was a precise, severe teacher. Gamaliel taught St. Paul. Hillel was known for his kindness. Scholar Henri Daniel-Rops believes that when Jesus visited Jerusalem as a child, he might have seen the gentle rabbi, Hillel, who died in 10 AD. The Mishna records what Hillel and Shammai taught, giving a glimpse of the thinking that formed Jesus as a teen.

Shammai said to make Torah study "a fixed duty, say little and do much, and receive every man with a cheerful face." Hillel taught that we should not judge a fellow man until we are in his place, and summarized Torah as telling us not to do to others what we would hate done to ourselves.

Herodians

Herodians were wealthy Jews, to whom Herod the Great had given lands to secure their loyalty. We know little about them, but Jesus often spoke disparagingly of rich landowners.

Zealots

The Zealots, an extremist sect, took root in Galilee in 6 AD under Judas of Gamala. Zealots believed in God's rule alone, and longed for the Messiah to free them from Roman rule and taxes. Never flinching at violence, they incited riots and assassinated their enemies, including other Jews who disagreed with them. Their revolt in 6 AD, which Jesus probably remembered, brought swift punishment from Rome.

Travel in Jesus' Day: Rugged Roads and Combative Samaritans

Everywhere Jesus went all his life, he walked. The main Holy Land roads ran in a north-south direction. Travelers, traders, and conquering armies most often used one in particular, a busy camel-caravan route for spices and exotic goods. It began in Babylon, Mesopotamia (today's southern Iraq), led through Damascus (Syria), passed through Galilee, ran south along the coast, and on into Egypt.

Remains of ancient Roman road along the "Ascent of Adummim," the route pilgrims walked from Jericho to Jerusalem's heights.

This trade highway placed the Holy Land on a crossroads of nations, which meant Jesus was exposed to different cultures. Moreover, the Roman conquerors worked continually on widening and maintaining roads throughout the Empire to benefit their speeding horsemen and chariots.

East-west roads and their branches crisscrossed the country, linking the major north-south routes and their branches. Many of the Holy Land's cities, towns, and villages were built near one of the rocky main roads or close to a well-beaten dirt path that connected to a main road. Long before he was a traveling teacher, teen Jesus knew these roads well, as did all Jewish pilgrims to Jerusalem.

Travel on foot was never easy in Jesus' time, but political and religious tensions made it worse. The fastest route between Nazareth in Galilee and Jerusalem in Judea was a north-south road through the

Photo Credit: Todd Bolen/BiblePlaces.com

hills of Samaria. Most Jewish pilgrims and travelers avoided this short-cut. Instead, they detoured *around* the Samaritans' territory, hiking the rugged Jordan Valley down to Jericho and then upward toward the capital.

Hostility between Jews and Samaritans began nearly 600 years before Jesus' time, when Babylon's King Nebuchadnezzar destroyed Solomon's **First Temple** and took Jerusalem's Jews captive. Left behind, Samaritans intermarried with incoming pagan settlers and followed their own version of the Hebrew Bible.

Unrest still exists in Samaria, known today as the West Bank of the River Jordan. Roughly 750 Samaritans remain there. They speak Arabic and ancient Hebrew. They have a high priest, worship in synagogues, sacrifice a Passover lamb on Mount Gerizim, and claim to be both Israeli and Palestinian.

Some fifty to seventy years later, King Cyrus of Persia defeated the Babylonians and allowed the Jews to return home. The exiles rebuilt a shabby version of the First Temple on Mount Moriah, which Herod the Great was transforming when Jesus was born. Historians don't always agree on exact dates, but around 332–329 BC, the Greeks arrived, led by Alexander the Great, conqueror of the then-known world.

The Samaritans got Alexander's permission to build their *own* temple on Mount Gerizim, near Shechem (today's city of Nablus)—where they believed Abraham brought his son Isaac for sacrifice and where Noah's ark had landed. This competing shrine to *Yahweh* infuriated the Jews so much that a Hasmonean prince destroyed it about 100 years before Jesus was born. Samaritans, however, continued to worship at the site.

Jesus ignored this mutual hatred when he spoke with the Samaritan woman at the well (John 4:1–42). He also shocked an audience of followers when the Good Samaritan in his parable did the unthinkable—he helped a Jew (Luke 10:25–37).

Under the Thumb of Foreign Conquerors: Greeks and Romans

When Jesus was born, Rome ruled the world. Caught in the Empire's tight fist, the Jewish people bristled. But earlier, Alexander the Great had conquered their region (332–329 BC) and spread his more tolerant Greek culture. In public marketplaces, foreign traders sold exotic goods carried by camels from the far reaches of the empire—and people bartered for them in Greek, the universal language.

Based on the Hebrew calendar and Herod's death in 4 BC, scholars think Jesus was born around 6 BC (suggested dates range from 3–7 BC). From April to October, mild Holy Land weather allows shepherds to sleep outdoors with their flocks.

Studies of ancient Babylonian astronomy reveal that in May, October, and December of 7 BC, Saturn and Jupiter passed so closely they appeared to be one brilliant star. During one of these times, Mars joined the other two planets. Did the Eastern magi see this dazzling event in the night sky as a sign of a royal birth in the region of the Holy Land?

Alexander had respected the different religions practiced by his many subjects. In fact, Josephus said, he sacrificed animals in the Temple to the Jewish God. But after Alexander's early death—only six years later, in 323 BC—his generals fought for pieces of the vast empire. Ptolemy ruled the land that stretched from Egypt to an area south of the Holy Land. His rival, Seleucus, established the Seleucid dynasty in Syria, to the north. The Holy Land was in the middle of their ongoing power struggle. Never known to be submissive, the Jews fought back and even sided with Romans, who were already in the region, against their common Seleucid enemy.

In 164 BC, nearly 200 years later, the Jewish **Maccabees** finally won independence from the Greek/Syrian oppression and founded the Hasmonean Dynasty, in which each king also assumed the high priesthood. But by 67 BC, two royal sons, Aristobul and Hyrcanus, were fighting one another for the throne. Rome, by then looking to expand their territory, intervened to settle the dispute and instill order in the region.

So it was that in 63 BC, General Pompey conquered Jerusalem and added the land of Judea to the Roman province of Syria, nearby. Like all Roman subjects, Jews were then heavily taxed and kept under military occupation. They were forced to accept yet another foreign culture: the Latin language, public baths, statues of idols, and coins engraved with images of emperors who claimed to be gods. Romans did not respect others' religions. Their pagan practices enraged the Jewish people, who rebelled often.

Herod the Great: Ruler from 37–4 BC

Destined for greatness, a young governor named Herod, one of Rome's regional puppet rulers, won the friendship of Mark Antony, whose later political and marital alliances with Cleopatra proved fatal. In 40 BC, Antony helped Herod be named the King of Judea. Backed by Rome, Herod fought Antigonus, the last Hasmonean king, and his allies. In 37 BC, Herod gained control of Jerusalem and the Jewish throne.

After Octavian, the future Caesar Augustus, defeated Antony and Cleopatra in the Battle of Actium in 31 BC, Herod quickly switched his loyalty to the victor. A shrewd politician and efficient money manager, Herod shared his wealth with Rome and stayed in power for more than thirty years.

A large-scale builder, Herod the Great constructed the sea-port city of Caesarea Maritima with a Greek-style theater and sports stadium, built the fortified palaces of Masada and Herodium in the desert, and took possession of Hyrcania, the Maccabees' existing desert fortress. His massive walls around Jerusalem, as well as the **Antonia Fortress**, added to the city's safety. In Jerusalem, he restored the luxurious Hasmonean palace and, with his own money, enlarged and rebuilt the Second Temple.

Herod, though King of Judea, was not born Judean. His father, Antipater II, belonged to an Arab tribe in Idumea, which is south of Judea, and had allied with Rome in *his* struggle against the Hasmoneans. Herod's mother, also of Arabic heritage, came from Petra in today's Jordan, then a wealthy trading center for myrrh and frankincense.

King Herod's family had earlier converted to Judaism under threat of death by Jewish conquerors, who made his grandfather a governor. Herod married a Hasmonean princess and practiced Judaism, but clashed constantly with the Hasmonean priests, who still eyed the throne. Likely because they opposed the ambitious priests and did not worship in the Temple, the Essenes sided with Herod. However, most Jews viewed Herod as a foreigner and rejected him as their rightful ruler.

Whispers of plots to overthrow the king swirled constantly. Suspicious and cruel, Herod ordered countless executions: political enemies, baby boys around Bethlehem, two of his ten wives, and so many of his sons that Emperor Augustus reportedly said it would be better to be one of Herod's pigs than to be his son. Jews don't eat pork, after all.

Herod's Death and a Jewish Revolt

As he lay dying, Herod imprisoned thousands of Jewish leaders and ordered them killed at news of his death to ensure public mourning. His sister ultimately showed mercy and freed the men. Nevertheless, after Herod's death, the Jews again revolted. Sweeping in from his base in nearby Syria, the Roman General Varus swiftly put down the uprising. He destroyed the rebels' chief city, **Sepphoris**, located near the village of Nazareth in Galilee.

Uprisings always attracted the Romans' attention. Fast. Rome gloried in its "Pax Romana," which is Latin for "Roman Peace." The Empire demanded that conquered territories be under control at all times and didn't hesitate to crush rebellions. Leaders who roused the people to revolt, an accusation later brought against Jesus, were publicly crucified as a warning to others. Despite such tyranny, riots remained common throughout the Holy Land.

After his death, three surviving sons of Herod the Great divided his kingdom. In Jerusalem, Archelaus ruled Samaria and Judea until 6 AD. After the people's protests about his cruelty, Rome banished him and placed the southern province under the direct authority of a Roman prefect, or governor. Pontius Pilate, who ruled Judea from 26–36 AD, would be Judea's fifth prefect.

Herod Philip ruled the region northeast of the Sea of Galilee. Herod Antipas reigned over Galilee and Perea, an area across the Jordan River. This was the King Herod who later beheaded John the Baptist and interrogated Jesus after his arrest. Antipas' rule ended in 39 AD, when the Romans exiled him.

Nazareth

After Herod the Great—who had decreed the slaying of young Jewish children in Bethlehem—died, Joseph and Mary returned from Egypt, bringing Jesus with them. Because Jerusalem was in turmoil, Joseph looked to Galilee, then ruled by Herod Antipas, as a safer place to live among relatives.

Mystery surrounds the Holy Family's exile in Egypt (Matthew 2:13–23). Monks of the Ethiopian Orthodox Christian Church still guard a shrine on an island in Lake Tana. Their ancient oral tradition says Jesus and Mary spent ten days there during their "four-year exile" in Egypt. Though unlikely, as Egypt is more than 1,000 miles from the shrine, the faithful hold fast to their beliefs, which no one can prove or disprove.
("Keepers of the Lost Ark?" *Smithsonian*, December 2007)

A builder like his father, Herod Antipas had decided to rebuild Sepphoris, left in ruins by Varus, and make it into the sophisticated capital of his domain. Four miles away, in the small village of Nazareth, Joseph settled his family. There Jesus grew up, his world overshadowed by an unpopular king and despised Roman conquerors. Moreover, within Judaism itself, there was turmoil as Hasmonean

Jesus' World

priests continued their ruthless quest for power and Zealots continued to riot against Rome. But Jesus was grounded—in his family, in God, and in Torah, the Law of Moses.

Questions for Discussion

1. Hard as it might be, try to imagine the United States invaded and occupied by an enemy. (During World War Two, many people thought it just might be possible that we would be conquered by Germany or Japan.) Who might that enemy be? How would it feel to go about your business under the eyes of watchful soldiers? What would you do? How would your life change?

2. Except for Native Americans, all our ancestors came here as foreigners or aliens; that is, people who were born in another country. What do you know about your cultural heritage? Do you still observe any customs from your forefathers' country (or countries) of birth? Do you know someone who lives in the United States now, but was born elsewhere? What did he/she need to do to become a citizen? How can embracing many different cultures enrich us and make us a stronger nation? What are some current issues regarding illegal aliens in our country?

FOUR

The House Joseph Built

Better is a dry morsel with quiet than a house full of feasting with strife.

—Proverbs 17:1

Mary (*Miriam* in Hebrew) was likely fourteen or fifteen when she became engaged to Joseph. When her pregnancy became obvious before the wedding, she faced the criminal charge of adultery. This might have meant a trial in the Temple, where she would have been forced to drink a bitter potion. Getting sick from the drink meant a woman was guilty and faced death by stoning. But Joseph, a godly man who wanted to spare her from this terrible punishment, decided to end the engagement quietly, with a written bill of divorce given before witnesses.

Mary knew people were talking about her and judging her, but she kept silent and trusted God to work out everything. He did. An angel came to Joseph in a dream and said, "Do not be afraid to take Mary as your wife, for the child conceived in her is from the Holy Spirit" (Matthew 1:20). Joseph's heroism not only saved Mary from being stoned, but it also saved the life of her unborn child.

Other than Jesus' infancy narrative—birth, circumcision, and presentation in the Temple—and his teaching in the Temple at age twelve, the Gospels say little about his boyhood. "The child grew and became strong, filled with wisdom; and the favor of God was upon him" (Luke 2:40) and "Jesus increased in wisdom and in years, and in divine and human favor" (Luke 2:52). He grew up as *Yeshua* ("*Yahweh* is salvation") *ben Yosef* or "Jesus, son of Joseph" in Hebrew.

Jesus' clan members were called **Nazoreans**, from the Hebrew word for "branch" (*nezer*), because they "sprouted" from the royal line of King David and his father, Jesse. After returning from the Babylonian Exile, some descendants of David's clan likely settled in Nazareth, a name that means "village of the branch." That would mean many if not most of Nazareth's residents belonged to one extended family, the Nazorean clan, sprung from King David's line.

What Was Nazareth Like?

People who lived in towns and cities usually protected themselves against intruders with high thick walls, set with a heavy gate that they barred shut at night. Not so in Nazareth. Inhabitants built their small village settlement on the slope of a basin that backed up to a ridge of limestone hills, using their natural formation as protection. Nazareth's height, 1,300 feet above sea level, gave breathtaking views of its surroundings, including a major road that wound through the Jezreel Valley, far below.

Any number of online sources help visualize how Jesus' world looked. For example, go to the Nazareth Village website at http://www.nazarethvillage.com. Click *Enter the Village* and *Archaeology* to see an excellent presentation of *The Houses*. You can also do key word searches for "Nazareth."

Water was vital for any village. Nazareth's well—still called "Mary's Well"—and a natural spring were located nearby. Archaeologists found no paved streets inside the small hillside village; worn footpaths likely wound throughout the settlement. Evidence of vineyards and farming still exists: terraces (steplike walls cut into the hills and faced with field stones) for grape vines, watchtowers, a winepress, fermenting vats, grinding stones, and storage pits dug into the stone to hold grain. Olive, fig, apricot, nut, pomegranate, and/or date palm trees probably grew in the village orchard.

Village Animals: Milk, Meat, and Clothing

Animals, too, were vital for village life and the rabbis urged kindness to them. People were to feed their herds before they themselves ate, allow work animals to rest on the Sabbath, yoke together an equal pair so one didn't pull a heavier load, not muzzle an ox while it plowed the fields (so it could eat), and own a work or companion animal only if they could feed it. Young Jesus might have untied the family's animals from mangers inside the compound and led them outside to drink every morning.

Did Jesus Have a Pet?

Often despised, most ancient dogs roamed free. However, people used some dogs to herd and protect sheep. Today's breed of Canaan dogs originally came from the Holy Land and might date back to biblical times. One ancient tradition says the apostle John told a story about Jesus that shows how deeply Jesus understood a child's bond with his dog. It also hints at great joy to come. The tradition goes like this:

> One day, Rabbi Jesus found a little boy crying beside his dead dog. Picking up the child, Jesus told him that animals are able to see what few people do. He then handed the boy a small seashell he'd found on the shore that morning. Jesus explained that, like the dog's lifeless body, it had once housed a living creature. The sea snail had outgrown its temporary home and moved on, leaving its empty shell behind. It had left but not died, Jesus assured the boy. It was living somewhere else, unseen by human eyes.

A Sonoma State University team made a 3-D facial reconstruction of an Arabic teenage boy who died 4,000 years ago and whose skeleton was found in a burial mound on the island of Bahrain. His startling beauty, brought to life with plastic and clay, reminds us of our shared humanity with people of the past. Draped around the bust is a piece of raw silk that is similar to ancient fabrics' "loose weave and slightly uneven texture." ("Face to Face with the Past," *Near Eastern Archaeology Magazine*, June 2012)

Traditional or apocryphal writings, like this religious legend, are not found in Scripture. However, those that ring true to Jesus' teachings and actions are accepted as supplemental because they contain *extra* information, rather than being rejected as false. Since some traditional stories might actually have happened, they are still passed on.

Village Homes: Built for Single and Extended Families

Throughout the Holy Land, archaeologists discovered traces of small single-family homes and larger compounds for extended families. In Nazareth, a simple two-room dwelling with a courtyard, as well as pottery fragments dated to Jesus' time, was recently excavated. Other remains of housing found in Nazareth include stone-lined storage pits, deep cisterns carved into the bedrock (to catch rain and channel runoff water from the roof gutters), and once-inhabited caves.

Caves abound in the region; people in Jesus' day often built their homes in front of them to extend living space. To the extent possible, exterior house walls were cut out of the hilly bedrock and built higher with layers of mortared stones. Builders left narrow open spaces high in the walls to serve as windows; these protected the family's privacy while letting in air and light. To form a standard flat roof, men laid wall-to-wall wooden beams and covered them with bundles of brush or overlapping mats made of branches. The roof was topped with thick layers of hard-packed clay. Written Torah advised adding a low wall around the sides for safety (Deuteronomy 22:8).

Jesus grew up in a large extended family, where members shared limited living space and cared for one another (Matthew 13:55–56). On returning from Egypt, Joseph may have chosen to build a simple, one-room "starter" home in Nazareth village.

In those days, it was common for an entire family to live in a single room probably measuring only about fifteen feet by fifteen feet. If no cave was nearby, a dugout or blocked-off area close to the door formed a stable. There, the family's farm animals spent cold nights, tied to a manger filled with crushed straw, and shared their body heat.

When families inevitably needed more space, a large compound began to grow. Before marrying, each son added a room onto his father's house, in which he, his wife, and their children lived. All the extra rooms—for living, storage, working, and sheltering animals—were built around a central courtyard, enclosing it for privacy.

Homes of wealthier families sometimes had two or three stories, which were supported by stone pillars. If a family compound did have a second story, the airy upper rooms served as living quarters. However, this was an exception to the rule.

Researchers have found the remains of a seventh-century BC royal garden at Ramat Rachel, near Jerusalem. Its once-lush area had an irrigation system with channels, tunnels, gutters, and waterfalls. Similar gardens in the Babylonian, Assyrian, and Persian kingdoms were set aside as places of serenity. Jesus' people loved "green" spaces!

Entry doors, which could be bolted shut, had a *mezuzah* (a tiny, rolled Scripture scroll inside a decorated case about 5"–7" by 1.5") hanging on the doorpost. Because dwellings had no inside bathrooms, people bathed and relieved themselves outdoors. Water was scarce and used sparingly, so Nazareth probably had one *mikveh*, which was shared by all the villagers.

Since Joseph had relatives already settled in Nazareth, it's possible he added yet another room onto one of their sprawling family compounds. If so, Jesus grew up in close quarters with many cousins, as well as his sisters and brothers. Whether he lived in a small single-family home or in a large extended-family compound, living space was scant. Jesus surely had no bedroom of his own—or any of the privacy we take for granted.

Cozy Inside

Layers of plaster, made of mud and straw, insulated the inside walls. To light the home's dim interior and to start their cooking fires, women kept a small clay oil lamp always burning in a wall niche or on a stand. Families stored their precious supply of well water, drawn daily by the women, in large covered limestone jars; we read in the Gospel of John (2:6) that each jar held twenty to thirty gallons. Like naturally flowing water, the white limestone common throughout the Holy Land was always **ritually pure**. Insects, snakes, and scorpions were a problem, so people also kept wine, oil, and flour in covered jars.

Photo Credit: Todd Bolen/BiblePlaces.com

An ancient Holy Land house, made of mud bricks and stones.

Pottery and household items recovered in Nazareth were plain and homemade. Though clay dishes were most common, families favored cups, plates, trays, and bowls made of "pure" white limestone or chalk. Copper, bronze, clay, or wooden vessels had to be ritually cleansed by immersion in water after use.

Perhaps Joseph made stools, shelves, and a wooden chest where Mary could store clothing, large casserolelike bowls for mixing ingredients and serving food, cooking pots, ladles, jugs, and vessels for eating and drinking. Her handwoven baskets were filled with dried fruit or nuts. Few other furnishings stood on their packed-earth floor, since only the rich could afford tables, couches, and beds.

People looked forward to warm weather, when they climbed a ladder or outer stairs to their flat rooftops. There, the women had extra room to spread fruit, grain, and laundry to dry. There, families gathered to eat together, work, study Scripture, and unroll their sleeping mats under the stars. Population estimates for Nazareth vary greatly. Whatever the number, it is generally agreed that about 400 people were crowded together on roughly ten acres of land. From their rooftop in this tiny village, Jesus' family could easily chat with nearby relatives, who were enjoying the fresh evening air on their adjacent rooftops.

Jewish Male Fashion: Tunic, Belt, Cloak, Tefillin, Turban

As Jesus dressed every morning, he blessed the Lord God, Who clothed him. Over his linen wraparound loincloth, he put on a homemade linen **tunic** or robe, which reached below the knees and had long wide sleeves. A modest Jewish man wore the tunic alone only when inside his house or if doing physical work outside.

To keep it from billowing, the tunic needed a belt or sash. This could be a piece of rope or a long folded piece of woven wool, linen, goat hair, or leather that wrapped around the waist several times, like a cummerbund. The belt's folds formed a purse or pouch, in which one could conceal and carry small items like coins, a knife, food, or dice.

To move freely, men reached between their knees, grabbed the back hem of their tunic, pulled it forward between their legs and up, tucking it into the front of their belt. This formed "girded loins." Jesus did this before working, running, or maybe wrestling with his brothers. He wore simple leather sandals. Archaeological evidence—a perforated footprint in a Holy Land cement wall—shows Roman soldiers wore hobnailed sandals.

In public, proper Jewish men wore a *tallit*—a fringed cloak or mantle, usually woven of wool, camel hair, or goat hair—over the tunic. The cloak reached below the knees and could be draped over one shoulder in Greek/Roman style, or closed in front with a clasp. A protection from rain and cold, it also served as a blanket. The *tallit* was so essential in so many ways that Moses' Law or Torah (Exodus 22:26–27) required that a poor man's cloak, given in pledge for a debt, had to be returned to him before nightfall.

Torah (Numbers 15:38–39) required Jewish men to wear knotted woolen **fringes** or tassels on each corner of their cloaks, to help them "remember all the commandments of the Lord and do them." The woman suffering from hemorrhages in Luke 8:44 is healed by simply touching Jesus' fringes. Most fringes were left natural white. One was dyed with *tekhelet*, a beautiful and expensive blue dye, because in Moses' vision of God "under his feet there was . . . a pavement of sapphire stone" (Exodus 24:10).

Authentic *tekhelet* could be obtained only from the secretions of hundreds of sea snails called *hilazons*. Over time, the hilazon's identity and the secret process of making *tekhelet* were lost. However, archaeologists found piles of broken shells from Murex sea snails, and a stained shard from a 3,200-year-old vat that matched Murex dye. Made outdoors, Murex dye turns purple on cloudy days, so precise exposure to sunlight was likely part of making two ancient dyes, *tekhelet* and royal purple. Purple cloth was so expensive only kings and nobles wore it.

By age thirteen, Jesus' community considered him a man. He then strapped *tefillin* (**phylacteries**) onto his forehead and arm. These small black leather boxes contained parchment scrolls inscribed with Scripture. Head tefillin had four compartments, each of which held one tiny scroll: a reminder to celebrate Passover, another to consecrate the firstborn, and the **Shema** (a prayer) divided into two parts. Jesus wrapped hand *tefillin* onto his "weaker" arm—his left, if he was right-handed. Hand *tefillin* had only one compartment with one scroll, unlike head *tefillin*'s four compartments and four scrolls.

Jewish men kept their hair shoulder length or shorter. One first-century tomb, discovered near Jerusalem, had skeletal remains of a man with reddish hair, evenly trimmed to three to four inches long. Torah forbade shaving the edges of one's beard. Jewish men probably took pride in growing their beards, since the Roman conquerors and occupiers of their land were clean-shaven. To protect his head from the heat, Jesus might have worn a turban or a long cloth headdress, tied at the forehead. The custom of Hebrew men wearing a *kippah* or *yarmulke* (fabric skullcap) came later.

Jewish women wore the same basic clothing as men, though their garments were likely ankle length. In Jesus' time, women had no religious obligation to add fringes to their cloaks or to wear the *tallit* required of men. Now, however, many Jewish women wear one for

Jewish boy, wearing head and hand phylacteries, praying at the Western Wall.

prayer. Men's cloaks were usually not dyed, except for the blue fringes, but left in the natural colors of the woven hair or wool. Women dyed their cloaks in vibrant colors. The rabbis taught that a married woman's hair, usually worn loose or braided, should always be covered as a mark of modesty. They did this with a corner of their cloak, a cap, hairnet, or scarf.

After dressing, teen Jesus poured water from a pitcher into a bowl and washed his face and hands over it, saving the precious supply for other uses, like watering the garden. He ate a light breakfast, perhaps bread or fruit with fresh goat's milk, cheese, or yogurt. Mary packed his lunch, which may have included toasted grain, dried fruit, olives, and cheese, before he left home for a day of work and study.

Now we'll discover how the world Jesus knew shaped what he did all day.

Questions for Discussion

1. Jesus' world, in an age when most people travelled by foot, was small and self-contained. What similarities would you find between his world and yours?

2. Think about living in a home as small as his. Then think about how different it was from yours. What might there be to like about a tiny house with a flat roof where you could hang out at night, visiting with your neighbors?

3. Do you have your own room or do you share? If you share a room, how do you keep from arguing over living space and personal belongings?

4. Water was (and still is) precious in desert lands. Not a drop is wasted. In the Middle East, Africa, India, Central America, Asia and other parts of the world, *clean* water is also scarce. We take it for granted that when we turn on a faucet, clean water will come out, just was we expect light to come on when we flip a switch. How would your life change if you suddenly found yourself without fresh water and electricity? What would you do about it?

FIVE

Inside Jesus' Home: Torah, Prayer, and Work

Upon three things the world stands: upon Torah, upon worship, and upon the showing of kindness.
—Mishna

Jesus and his family belonged to the Chosen People, the only ones at that time who worshipped One God and followed the Covenant, or agreement, that God made with Abraham centuries before: "I will . . . be God to you and to your offspring" (Genesis 17:7).

Some 500 years later, Moses led the Jewish people—descendants of Abraham, Isaac, and Jacob—out of Egypt. On Mount Sinai, God spoke from a thick cloud. "If you obey my voice and keep my covenant, you shall be my treasured possession" (Exodus 19:5). There, amid smoke and thunder, he dictated to Moses the Ten Commandments, plus 613 more commands. During forty years in the desert, Moses taught his people these guides for right living, known as the Law of Moses or Torah, which means "teaching."

Not all the 613 Commandments carried the same weight. However, said the rabbis, every law was binding—from one that was "heavy" (required serious effort, like honoring parents), to one that was "light" (easily obeyed, like eating only the eggs from a nest, not the mother bird). Rabbis also urged joy in carrying out all God's laws.

Written Torah: Genesis, Exodus, Leviticus, Numbers, Deuteronomy

The Bible's first five books, called the Five Books of Moses, preserve the Ten Commandments and 613 other commandments Jews are bound to obey. They are called Written Torah or Written Law. But Torah went beyond following a series of dry rules.

In *The Spiral Staircase*, Karen Armstrong writes that following Torah *brought God* into every moment of a Jew's life; simple acts (such as dressing, washing, eating) became opportunities to meet the Divine. Studying Torah, she adds, worked the other way; it *brought the people* "into the presence of God." Every Jew loved Torah and strove to deepen his understanding of it. Since the first five books of Scripture are the same in the Christian Bible and the Hebrew Bible, which Christians call the Old Testament, scholars know what Written Torah contained. But there was much more to the Law.

Men holding up a revered Torah scroll at the Western Wall in Jerusalem.

Oral Torah and the Mishna

Rabbis interpreted and explained Scripture or Written Torah for the people. They voiced many different opinions about how Torah said to live the ideal life. The rabbis' explanations of Written Torah were called Oral Torah or Oral Law. Oral Torah was still unwritten in Jesus' time, but we have an idea what it said.

By 200 AD, the Jewish people, persecuted and scattered in exile, feared losing their oral traditions forever. Rabbi Judah Hanasi, called a "prince" or *nassi* (head of his community), began to organize and write down Oral Torah. After he died, other Jewish scholars continued his work, called the Mishna.

Completed around 500–600 AD, the Mishna contained six **seders**, which is Hebrew for six orders or categories: Food and Blessings, Sabbath and Festivals, Women, Damages, Temple Rituals, and Ritual Purity. Each seder was subdivided into long **tractates**. Each of the sixty-three tractates was subdivided into chapters. The Mishna—plus stories, meditations, and commentary on the six orders by yet *more* rabbis—makes up the enormous body of Jewish religious and civil laws, traditions, and commentary known today as the **Talmud**.

The Mishna recorded Oral Torah from 200 years *before* Jesus' time and 200 years *after* Jesus' time. But because Oral Law was in flux for centuries, experts don't know (and can't know) how much of its present form existed in Jesus' day. However, most agree the Mishna contains the *essence* of the Oral Torah Jesus studied.

Prayer

Studying Torah taught Jews to be aware of God's presence and grateful for everything in our world. Prayer, however, helped them *touch* God. Prayer started each day and made it sacred. As soon as Jesus and his family woke every morning, they thanked God for returning their souls to them, just as he would restore their bodies at the resurrection of the dead. They were happy to be alive, since the Jewish sages taught that sleep was "one-sixtieth of death."

Jews knew their eternal God as *Yahweh*—"LORD/I AM." Hands raised, they stood when they prayed, facing Jerusalem and the Temple. In prayer or study, silently or aloud, the people respectfully substituted other names, like **Shaddai** ("Almighty") or **Ha-Shem** ("The Name"). Jesus used "Heaven" (Luke 15:21) and "Power" (Matthew 26:64).

God's four-letter Unutterable Name, written *YHWH* or Y_H_W_H, sounds like breathing when spoken: *Yhhh . . . Whhh . . .* That's why God is called the Breath of Life. Only priests were allowed to say the full name aloud and only in the Temple, a place holy enough to contain its power. In *The Complete Idiot's Guide to the Talmud*, Rabbi Aaron Parry mentions a powerful, mysterious forty-two-letter name for God. Never written down, it was lost when the Temple was destroyed and the priesthood ended.

We still use some ancient Hebrew words Jesus used in prayer and worship: **Amen** ("Truly!" or "We agree, this is the truth!"), *Hosanna* (a shout of joyous praise to God), and **Alleluia** ("Praise God!" from *hallelu* and *Yah*—the first half of *Yahweh*). Devout Jews still write "G-d," rather than the entire Holy Name.

When God was seen as strict, the Jewish people called him **Elohim**—a word that has a masculine ending, suggesting Father. When God was seen as merciful, they called Him **Adonai**—which means "Lord," but has a feminine ending, suggesting Mother.

During the day, Jesus and his family often raised their minds and hearts to God. They "blessed" (praised and thanked) him for all that he gave and in all circumstances. Prayers of petition weren't meant to change God's mind, but to change or transform the one who encountered God. Torah also required formal prayers, including the ancient and beautiful **Amidah** and *Shema*.

The *Amidah* and the *Shema*

The *Amidah*—Hebrew for "standing"—is the central prayer in Jewish life and liturgy. Every Jewish man, from age thirteen and up, was obliged to recite its three Scripture passages, which began with "Blessed are you, O Lord." In Jesus' time, the *Amidah* was said twice a day—standing straight and tall, both feet together—and consisted of the Eighteen Blessings: prayers of praise, petition, and thanks. Because of household duties and childbearing, says Rabbi Shmuel Safrai, women were excused from Torah study and specific prayer times. But because prayer was an "obligation of the heart," women were required to pray the formal *Amidah* or a short prayer of thanks.

The *Shema*, the Jewish declaration of faith, came from Written Torah and was recited every morning and evening. The first of its three parts is familiar, because Jesus called it the greatest commandment:

> Hear, O Israel: the LORD is our God, the LORD alone. You shall love the LORD your God with all your heart, and with all your soul, and with all your might. Keep these words that I am commanding you today in your heart. Recite them to your children and talk about them when you are at home and when you are away, when you lie down and when you rise. Bind them as a sign on your hand, fix them as an emblem on your forehead, and write them on the doorposts of your house.
>
> —Deuteronomy 6:4–9

Because of Torah's command, men's *tefillin* or phylacteries held tiny rolled scrolls inscribed with Scripture, including part of the *Shema*. Tiny Scripture scrolls were also placed inside the *mezuzah* on the doorpost. Jewish families still respectfully touch the *mezuzah* when they enter or leave their homes, just as Jesus' family did.

When Jesus prayed and spoke, he likely used different languages. Rabbi Shmuel Safrai says that, although ancient Jews knew and spoke Aramaic, Hebrew was the "dominant spoken and written language." Written Torah was read in formal Hebrew, but "conversation, prayer and Oral Torah" were in a dialect called Mishnaic Hebrew. Some scholars wonder if Jesus and Pontius Pilate spoke in Greek, then the universal language.

Love Ruled

Torah said God should always be welcome in a Jewish home. A Jewish mother, the heart of the home, taught her children to obey Torah's commandments and to perform *mitzvot*, good deeds and acts of kindness. Honor—personal, family, and village honor—strongly bound Jews to the religious obligation of offering hospitality (food, drink, and shelter) to traveling rabbis and strangers. Failure to act rightly brought shame/disgrace.

Honor still binds Middle Easterners to protect guests. One retired pastor and Holy Land traveler told how a Palestinian family, pursued by Israeli soldiers, begged a Jewish merchant for help. Moved by pity, he hid them in the back of his shop and served them coffee. Soon the soldiers burst into the shop—and the merchant served *them* coffee. He then revealed the family, insisting that everyone who had drunk his coffee was his guest. The soldiers left and the family continued their flight, safe passage assured.

Within Middle Eastern families, relatives extended kindness and affection to one another. In Jesus' day, frequent kissing was common among parents, children, cousins, and friends. Some kisses were required, as when welcoming a guest into one's home. People who had superior status in society might kiss a person of lesser stature to show kindness, while the lower class man or woman would kiss his master's hand or feet to show respect. Jesus would have shared in all this open affection.

Jewish mothers especially loved their sons and even pampered them. Their close bond lasted for life, as adult sons had the responsibility of caring for their aging mothers. Before starting school at age five, Jesus and other little boys spent their days under the watchful eyes of the women in the family: mothers, aunts, grandmothers, sisters, and girl cousins. What Jesus saw and experienced, including his years spent in the women's compound, carried over to his adult life and teachings.

What Women Did All Day

In cities, tradesmen milled flour, baked bread, dyed cloth, and wove clothing. But in rural settlements like Nazareth, women did all this and more. During the spring and fall harvests, when grain and grapes were picked and processed, the entire village shared in the extra work.

Mary's day began before sunrise, when she rose, prayed, and dressed. To escape the day's heat, she and the other women left home early and walked to the village well, where they drew water and carried it back home in jugs, balanced on their heads.

Women and girls of all ages shared the household work, doing chores together inside their family compound's walled, open-air courtyard. There, toddlers and small children played, sheep and goats bleated, dogs barked, and babies cried. There stood the family's beehive-shaped earthen oven, fueled by dried and salted animal dung and sticks, where fresh bread baked every day except the Sabbath.

Photo Credit: David Dorsey/BiblePlaces.com

Holy Land women during harvest, cutting and bundling sheaves of grain by hand.

Savory smells filled the air as the evening dinner, often a well-spiced vegetable stew, simmered for hours in a large pot that hung over a stone-lined fire pit and was sheltered under a lean-to. Cooking outside kept the house free of smoke.

Weaving, Laundry, and Making Meals from Scratch

Mary also spun fibers from flax plants into linen thread and spun sheared sheep coats into woolen yarn. Most she left in their natural colors or bleached them white. Some she dipped in pots of natural dye (yellow from the saffron crocus, crimson from an insect that lived on oak trees). With her handspun threads and yarns, she wove all her own family's clothing on a large standing loom, kept in the courtyard. She hand-wove sleeping mats from fresh straw. She scrubbed dirty clothes clean on a large rock, using pumice, lather from crushed soapwort plant leaves, or lye soap made from wood ashes.

Milked by hand into a large bowl, village goats provided fresh milk to drink. Leftover milk quickly soured and thickened into another food, yogurt. Women also poured milk into an animal skin pouch and swung it back and forth continually for an hour or two. This separated the milk's watery liquid (whey) from the curds (similar to cottage cheese). Dried and salted, curds became a fetalike cheese.

Mary prepared delicious hot main meals, such as soup, porridge, and stew. Afterward, she purified any bowls or utensils not made of "pure" limestone, but of clay or wood, by immersing them in water. Jewish women spiced their foods with salt from the Dead Sea, cinnamon, anise, coriander (cilantro), cumin, dill, saffron, "hyssop" (thought to be capers), mint, sesame and mustard seed. Women also helped weed and water the village vegetable garden, where flavorful garlic, leeks, onions, lentils, chickpeas, and watermelons grew. They watched and replenished their household supply of precious olive oil, which they used for burning in lamps, cooking, healing wounds, and moisturizing the family's skin and hair.

Mary pressed figs and raisins into small cakes, perhaps adding nuts and sesame seeds. She made a sweetener, also called "honey," by boiling dates or figs in water, straining the pulp, and cooking the syrup until it thickened into jam. Sometimes she quick-fried simple cakes and thin wafers on a flat heated stone or on a clay griddle, placed over stones in the fire pit. But her most time-consuming task was making bread.

"Give Us This Day Our Daily Bread"

Nazareth's silos show the villagers grew and stored grain. Barley grew in rocky soil and needed less water and time to ripen; in markets, it was more readily available and cheaper to buy than wheat. Wheat grain made the finest loaves, but was expensive. Jesus' mother prob-ably made her bread mostly from barley grain, or from a mixture of different cereal grains. But first, women had to pound each measure of grain into flour.

To begin, Mary put grain into a mesh sieve and shook it to remove pebbles, chaff, and straw. Then she and another woman sat on the ground, opposite one another, and poured the grain into a hole in the center of a large, heavy grinding stone. They spun the flat upper stone against the lower, hollowed-out stone to grind grain into flour. Jewish women spent as long as three hours making enough flour for bread to feed five people.

Next came the dough, which Mary made by mixing flour with water, salt, olive oil, and leaven—a piece of raw dough, old enough to have formed "sourdough" yeast in it. Yeast bread took several hours to rise. Mary then kneaded the risen dough by hand, shaped it into round loaves (similar to pita), and finally baked it in the clay oven.

Jesus Remembered the Bustling Courtyard

According to custom, Jesus lived under his mother's care until he reached Jewish "manhood" at age thirteen, when he left the women's world behind and took on adult responsibilities. But he never forgot that sheltered world of women and children. As a rabbi, he used familiar details from common everyday life to explain Scripture. In that way, women and children, as well as men, could relate to his stories.

For example, he told his followers to be the "salt of the earth." Salt drew blood from meat, making it ritually pure and fit to eat. Also, as wood was scarce, the village girls flattened animal dung into sun-dried and salted patties for fuel. Fresh salt layers placed on the bottom of the oven helped the dung burn better. Rather than meaning "salt" only as a flavoring or preservative, Jesus may have meant "salt" as a purifier or catalyst.

In the Gospels, he taught us to pray for "our daily bread," what we need for today and nothing more. He spoke of shepherds, vineyards, oil lamps, mustard seeds, coins, harvesting wheat, and fighting weeds. All these things the people understood, because he was talking about their everyday lives. But before Jesus became a learned rabbi, he had to go to school and master Torah.

Questions for Discussion

1. While men and older boys in Jewish families worked in the fields or at a trade, the women, girls, and young boys shared household chores. How does your family divide chores? What are your responsibilities? What do you hate to do? What do you enjoy doing?

2. It is in the Jewish tradition to pray regularly throughout the day. When is your favorite time to pray? What is your favorite place to pray? What exactly *is* prayer?

3. Jesus lived every moment centered in God's love. What can we do to hear God's quiet voice in the midst of our noisy lives?

SIX

Jesus' Synagogue School: Written Torah and Oral Torah

A person who repeats his lesson 100 times is not to be compared with him who repeats it 101 times.

—Talmud

For the Jewish people, study of the Law or Torah was considered one of the highest forms of worship. Torah study took place at home and in the synagogue, where the villagers gathered to hear a teacher or visiting rabbi read Scripture aloud, explain it, and answer their questions. The synagogue's assembly hall also served as a daily elementary school for village boys—and as an adult "house of study" for men and women (thirteen and older) on the Sabbath and Jewish holidays.

Usually, a synagogue was built on a town's highest point, with its entrance facing Jerusalem. Archaeologists excavated what appears to be a synagogue, dated later than Jesus' time. The rectangular building had one entrance that showed men and women entered together, columns, and a large *mikveh* nearby. Remains of synagogues found at other sites had rows of stone benches along two walls.

According to the Mishna, a teacher should have no more than twenty-five boys in his class. The rabbis also suggested that boys study Written Torah from the ages of five to ten and Oral Torah from ages ten to thirteen.

Synagogue at Herodium (one of Herod's palaces), with stone benches along three sides.

If this was so in Nazareth, by age thirteen Jesus had attended the strict synagogue school for eight years. Inside its walls, all silliness was forbidden, as were eating, sleeping, and using it as a shelter from bad weather. Boys were there for one thing—to learn Torah, the Law of Moses that was already more than 1,000 years old when Jesus was born.

Written Torah: Memorizing Every Word

From the age of five to ten, Jesus and other little boys sat on floor mats around their teacher. The teacher read his class Written Torah (the first five books of Scripture) from the synagogue's Torah scrolls, hand-copied by scribes. Because some scrolls were more than 100 feet long, they were wound around wooden cylinders with handles. Since Hebrew is written from right to left, a reader unrolled a biblical scroll with his left hand, read a Scripture passage, and rolled up what he'd finished reading with his right hand.

What did Jesus learn from Written Torah? Genesis tells the story of creation and continues to the story of Joseph, son of Jacob. Exodus speaks of Moses, Passover, the flight from Egypt, and the Ten Commandments. Leviticus covers laws regarding holiness and worship. Numbers describes the forty-year journey through the desert to the Promised Land. Deuteronomy contains the Law of Moses—his words and his death. The boys had no books, so they listened intently as their teacher read to them.

Ancient Hebrew was written without any vowels or punctuation marks. Hebrew words were built on three-letter roots or stems. For example, says Steven Notley, the word written as "S-PH-R" could be "book" (SePHeR), "story" (SiPuR), or "scribe" (SoPHeR). Changing a vowel changed a word's meaning. Teachers precisely pronounced each syllable, so boys correctly understood every word. Accuracy was vital in passing on the Law. Students repeated what they heard, chanting the Torah verses aloud, over and over, until they learned them so well they could recite them by heart.

Since Scripture was memorized, it was once thought only gifted Jewish boys learned to read and write. But archaeologists have discovered an "alphabet stone," dated to King Solomon's time. That find supports the opinion that many boys learned to read and write, beginning with the Hebrew alphabet—twenty-two letters, from *aleph* to *taf.* In fact, archaeologists found inkpots and pottery shards once used for writing practice. Also, some of the ancient wooden writing tablets were coated with beeswax, so inscriptions made with a stylus could be easily erased by smoothing the wax.

Oral Torah and the Mishna's Six Seders or Orders

From ten to thirteen, Jesus likely studied Oral Torah—the rabbis' hairsplitting debates about the meaning of Written Torah (Moses' Law) and their recommendations for how to act, based on the Law. Oral Torah also included the rabbis' wise sayings, traditional stories or parables, and legal rulings on different controversies. We turn to the six orders of the Mishna, Oral Torah in written form, for an *idea* of what Jesus learned at this age.

Some ancient cultures still pass on their traditions orally to each generation. On Cyprus, a Mediterranean island, about 1,000 Maronites (Lebanese Syrian Christians) speak an unwritten hybrid Aramaic language from Jesus' day. The Maronites made up an alphabet based on the sounds of 3,000 words and are putting together a dictionary.

The Mishna's first order, "Food and Blessings," recorded Jewish prayer, different blessings, and when and where to say them. The people knew they couldn't "bless" God. For them, the word meant "praise and thanks." Anne Punton writes that the root *(b-r-kh)* of the word *berakhah* (**blessing**) hints at bowing or bending *berekh* (the knee). Jews believed all blessings came from God and that he brought good from everything that happened, good and bad.

The first order also listed dietary laws called ***kashrut***, meaning "kosher" or "fit," that told the people what they could or couldn't eat. "Clean" animals chewed cud and had cloven hooves: sheep, goats, cattle, and oxen. Pigs, rabbits, and camels were considered "unclean;" their meat, especially pork, was forbidden. Because sheep and goats were valued for their milk and wool/hair, Jewish families seldom ate fresh meat—though both meat and fish could be dried, salted, or smoked. Meat and dairy could not be mixed.

For a celebration, a herd animal free of injury was ritually slain, washed and salted to remove all its blood, and roasted. Torah forbade the people to consume blood, a creature's life force (Leviticus 17:14). Kosher slaughtering required serious training in Jewish law, a sharp sacrificial knife, and great skill to cut across the animal's throat quickly and deeply. Loss of consciousness soon followed, making this method of slaughter the one considered most humane and—because blood drained completely—kosher. (Muslim *halal*, or guidelines for permitted foods, also calls for slaughtering animals this way.)

Locusts were the only kosher insects. Some cultures still eat large grasshoppers, either after fire roasting them or baking them in a hot oven. They could also be dried, powdered, and made into "biscuits" that tasted something like shrimp chips.

Fowl and their eggs were kosher. Jews raised pigeons in dovecotes—underground caves with small niches carved into the rock to hold bird eggs. Scavenger birds, like vultures and crows, and birds of prey were taboo, along with frogs and snakes. Dried sardines were common food. Fresh fish were available only near the Jordan River or Sea of Galilee. Kosher fish had to have fins and scales; therefore, eels, shellfish, and bottom-feeding catfish were forbidden.

Kosher foods also included fresh and dried fruits and fruit juice, vegetables, and nuts. Grains were "neutral" foods, as long as they were free of insects.

The Mishna's second order, "Sabbath and Festivals," appointed *Shabbat* as a day of rest, honoring the belief that God had rested on the seventh day of the week, after creating the world. On the Jewish Sabbath, which is the Christian Saturday, even the spirit of work was avoided. People had the entire day free from chores to rest, study Torah in the synagogue and at home, and enjoy leisurely discussions over family meals.

Besides Torah study, synagogues likely had other uses. The Theodotus Inscription, a first-century limestone tablet carved in Greek letters and found in a Jerusalem cistern, suggests a local synagogue had rooms and baths for pilgrims.

Jews also broke their work routine during the year to celebrate their holidays, which were the major religious festivals or feasts: Passover and Unleavened Bread, Pentecost, Trumpets, Tabernacles, Day of Atonement, Lights, and Lots.[1]

---

1. See chapters 8 and 9 for a description of feasts and festivals.

The third order, "Women," dealt with women's rights and family law. Men and women were considered equal before God, but had different responsibilities in marriage. A husband had to love and honor his wife, provide her necessities, and pay her a wedding dowry for support in case of his death or a divorce.

The fourth order, "Damages," pertained to fair business practices, injuries, losses, loans, property, inheritance, Sanhedrin (court proceedings), and punishment.

The fifth order, "Temple Rituals," included laws concerning holiness. This included "buying back" a firstborn male child from God with five silver coins, paid in the Temple. Jesus was forty days old when his parents took him to Jerusalem to "redeem" him from God, who claimed every firstborn as his own (Exodus 13:2). At eight days old, Jesus had received his name from Joseph and undergone circumcision to share in the physical "sign of the covenant" required of all Hebrew males. Jews were required to sacrifice the male firstborn of their cattle, sheep, and goats.

Bathing and cleanliness, especially frequent hand washing, were common Jewish practices. **The Mishna's sixth order**, "Ritual Purity," referred to ceremonial, as opposed to practical, cleanliness. Spiritual purification was required before entering the Temple and after touching blood, a corpse, a leper, an animal carcass, or other body fluids like spit. Ritual cleansing meant total immersion in the stepped bath, or *mikveh*.

Cut from bedrock and plastered over, a *mikveh* had to contain at least 150–200 gallons of "pure" water in order to cover a man's entire body. Rainwater ladled from a **cistern** qualified as pure, but rabbis preferred that a *mikveh* be filled with "living water," which flowed by gravity from natural sources, like springs. The water in a *mikveh* had to last from the end of the rainy season in March to the start of the next one in October. People might have bathed first, before ritual immersion, to keep the water clean.

Large mikveh *found south of the Temple Mount in Jerusalem.*

Wisdom of the Mishna

The Mishna's wisdom is still relevant in many aspects of life today. It is interesting to note that Louis Pasteur began his research in immunization after reading a reference in the Mishna, where the rabbis suggested that anyone bitten by a dog with rabies should eat a lobe of that dog's liver. Somehow, they knew that weak exposure to certain bacteria could stimulate the immune system to resist future infections. The sages also noted the health benefits of eating garlic—and advised people not to overeat.

Becoming a Proper Jewish Man

Jesus grasped both Written and Oral Torah well. In Matthew 5:17, he said he had come to *fulfill* the Law. At age twelve, Jesus questioned the Temple rabbis about their teachings, and "all who heard him were amazed at his understanding and his answers" (Luke 2:47). Was Jesus' questioning of these learned men rude behavior?

No. It was allowed and even expected that a young man interrupt and question a teacher's interpretation of Scripture. In fact, a "questions and answer" approach was how the rabbis taught in Jesus' time. Even the youngest in the community was encouraged to participate in discussions, voice opinions, and argue one's case regarding Scripture teachings.

The word *bar* is Aramaic for "son of," while *ben* is its Hebrew equivalent. Mark 10:46–52 tells us the blind beggar is named Bartimaeus, or son of Timaeus. In more recent times, David Ben-Gurion was the first prime minister of Israel. A Jewish boy becomes a "son of the commandment" or a *bar mitzvah* at age thirteen. A Jewish girl becomes a "daughter of the commandment" or a *bat mitzvah* at age twelve.

Formal education in Torah ended for most boys around age thirteen, when they began working in the fields or learned a trade from their fathers. When twelve-year-old Jesus slipped away from his parents to seek out Jerusalem's rabbis, was he already distancing himself from the women's world—showing he was no longer a child, but a man, ready to take responsibility for himself and his actions?

What about Jewish Girls?

Though Jewish girls did not receive a formal education, they heard rabbis teach Torah in the synagogue, and heard their fathers and brothers repeat it often at home. By the age of twelve, a girl was considered morally responsible for keeping the Law. She became a "woman" at puberty and usually married then, leaving her childhood home to join the household of her husband's father—with hopes of increasing his family with many sons.

First-century adult Jewish women were religious equals of men. They attended synagogue services, which included Torah reading and instruction, and participated in Bible sessions in the synagogue's house of study. But they weren't allowed to read publicly from Scripture.

Remembering the Spoken Word: Early Christians and the Gospels

The Jewish people preserved Torah by passing it orally from one generation to the next. How were they able to remember so much? First, they were trained from childhood to memorize what they heard. Second, just as you remember the verses to your favorite songs or rap because you love the music, Jesus loved Scripture. Like other rabbis, he lost himself in it. It was part of who he was and he knew every word of it by heart.

After thirty years of observation in Jesus' part of the world, Kenneth Bailey did a study that found Middle Eastern village elders "in the recent past" commonly transmitted long oral histories. These storytellers added, subtracted, or changed the order of details—but *not the story itself*. Listeners heard their traditions repeated often enough that they recognized and openly corrected major discrepancies.

During the early days of the church, the apostles told Jesus' story, preaching the "good news" of salvation in Hebrew and Aramaic. Most of their listeners were Jewish, accustomed to learning Torah by memory. Most had never seen Jesus, but they trusted the apostles as elders to repeat his sayings and miracles accurately, to interpret his teachings rightly, and to answer their questions as he would have done. Two ancient writers, Papias and Justin Martyr, describe the Gospels read in Sunday gatherings as the apostles' "memoirs."

The Four Gospels and the "Lost" Gospels

Around 65–95 AD, the four evangelists—Matthew, Mark, Luke, and John—wrote down in Greek, then the universal language, the eyewitness accounts of Jesus' sayings and miracle stories that were most widely used and best reflected what Jesus' mainstream followers remembered. In other words, they recorded the stories that sounded most like what Jesus would have said and done. Why is this important?

In those beginning years of Christianity, there was no central organized "church" or "faith," only communities of Jesus' followers widely scattered across the Middle East. This resulted in a range of religious viewpoints—not surprising in the Jewish world of questioning and debate. Even Peter and Paul had opposing opinions about the need for **Gentile** converts to be circumcised (Galatians 2:11–14).

As these different groups struggled to understand what their faith meant, they circulated other gospel stories. It is believed that there are at least twenty to thirty "lost gospels." Some narratives hinted of fantasy; for example, in *The First Gospel of the Infancy*, Jesus miraculously fixes Joseph's carpentry mistakes. Gnostics claimed to know Jesus' "secret" traditions.

The early church considered the lost gospels, which were written later than the Gospels in the New Testament, to be outside mainstream thought. For most believers, the stories of Matthew, Mark, Luke, and John rang true to Jesus' teachings—and, after many years, the early church accepted those Gospels as divinely inspired.

Each of the four evangelists emphasized a different aspect of Jesus' life. Mark, Peter's companion, wrote during the time that Christians were being fed to lions in Rome and described Jesus as the Suffering Messiah. Matthew gave us Jesus' Jewish ancestry and showed how he fulfilled God's promises to the Jewish people. Luke, Paul's Gentile companion, wrote about Jesus' compassion and saving death for all people. John described Jesus as the living Word of God.

Translating the four Gospels into Greek so more people could understand them was a huge challenge. At times, no Greek words conveyed exactly the same meaning as certain Hebrew or Aramaic words. Another big problem was translating Hebrew's hundreds of idioms—expressions that mean something other than what the words imply (like "catch a bus"). David Bivin gives one example: "The two men met with four eyes" means they were face to face with no one else present. When phrases like this were translated literally, they lost the imagery they conveyed—and caused confusion.

However, in spite of language difficulties, scholars who compare the earliest-known Scripture manuscripts with today's Bible say the four Gospels are *essentially the same memoirs of the apostles* that were read aloud whenever and wherever early Christians assembled to pray and celebrate the Last Supper. For more than 2,000 years, Jesus' story has remained intact, the heart or core of the Gospels preserved by his first Jewish disciples. The Bible is truly the living Word of God.

Questions for Discussion

1. *Madrasa* is an Arabic word for school. Usually, it means a private religious school where Muslim boys learn to read and write using *only* the Quran. They memorize their Holy Book by repeating its verses countless times, the way Jewish boys learn the Hebrew Bible in a synagogue. Girls were excluded from this intensive religious education. Assuming that situation in our day and in this country, what advantages to you see in this kind of study? What are the drawbacks? How would such an intensive concentration affect your life?

2. Over time, translations of the Bible have been changed and updated. A quick look at the King James Bible with the pronouns "thee" and "thou" and other antiquated language is a good example of the extent of changes over the years. How do you read the Bible differently now than you did as a child? What stories did you like then and what stories are you not so crazy about now?

3. What Bible stories make you angry or sad? What stories make you happy or exultant?

SEVEN

Jesus and Joseph: A Team in Perfect Sync

Hear, my child, your father's instruction, and do not reject your mother's teaching.

—Solomon's Proverbs 1:8

When he turned thirteen, Jesus left the women's courtyard and the children's elementary school to take his place in the adult male world, a world of serious Torah study and hard work. He came from a devout family, where he would have worked outside the home with his father and brothers, and studied Scripture at home with them. Moreover, as Jewish men studied and debated Torah together in their village synagogue, Jesus honed his skills.

Brilliant young rabbis-in-training commonly left home to study with a master teacher. As a teen, Josephus spent three years in the wilderness as a disciple of a holy man before he became a Pharisee. In John 7:14–15, we read that Jesus had "never been taught." But Jesus replied, "My teaching is not mine, but his who sent me" (John 7:16). Jesus taught with great authority, which suggests he studied hard to learn the Law, but always kept his heart open to Divine inspiration.

Joseph's example and guidance was crucial in teen Jesus' life. According to custom, Jewish fathers taught their sons to pray, work, accept pain and physical discipline in silence, live according to the Law of Moses, and protect their family honor. Boys learned to aim quick, sharp answers at anyone who tried to shame them. Middle Easterners still esteem honor so highly that secrecy, evasiveness, and even lies are acceptable ways for someone of that culture to save face.

However, Torah forbade falsely accusing others and swearing (calling God to witness) that a known falsehood was true. People only swore when telling the actual truth, which is why Jesus often added an oath to his teachings: "Amen, Amen, I say to you . . ." It was like saying, "Truly, truly, I'm not lying. This is the truth."

Tons of Homework

Jesus knew he wanted to be a teacher—and what he had to do to obtain that goal. The Mishna suggests that, from ages fifteen to eighteen, Jesus tackled the monumental task of learning Jewish civil and religious law—the rabbis' multiple rulings on different legal cases and on every possible situation. These include detailed arguments for and against a position, and show the rabbis' widely varying interpretations of Written Torah.

For example, Rabbi Aaron Parry explains the Mishna's fourth seder/order, Damages, by using a law in Written Torah: "If the ox gores a male or female slave, the owner shall pay to the slave owner thirty **shekels** of silver" (Exodus 21:32).

Starting with this requirement for the ox's owner to take responsibility for a slave's death, the rabbis expanded it. In their arguments, they saw the slave's death as preventable. Because oxen are capable of causing injury, the rabbis ruled that owners need strong fencing around dangerous animals. They addressed the *possibilities* of harm that might arise from an owner's animals, property hazards such as a deep pit, actions or failure to act, and how he should pay for damages that he should have foreseen.

This was only one of countless rulings Jesus had to know as a rabbi. Teachings based on exploring Scripture—like the ox case, which was a practical application of the Law to everyday life—were called *midrash* ("search" or "seek") *halakah*.

In all probability, Jewish students were expected to memorize Scripture/Written Torah exactly, word for word. However, Richard Bauckham writes that understanding "key statements" in other material was sufficient. In either case—memorizing passages or assimilating concepts—teen Jesus mastered Jewish law. But there was more.

Jesus immersed himself in memorizing *midrash haggadah*, the oral collection of Jewish literature, which is composed of parables, legends, and homilies. Rabbis used storytelling to expand on Scripture, illustrate a law, or simplify an idea. Jesus learned to become a great storyteller who used familiar picture words and real-life situations to hold his listeners' interest.

For example, Jews believed wealth was God's reward for living a good life. But in the story of the wealthy man who built new barns for his crops, expecting to enjoy life, Rabbi Jesus startled his listeners with the unexpected: "This very night your life is being demanded of you. And the things you have prepared, whose will they be?" (Luke 12:13–21). Jesus was saying, "Don't get too comfortable here. This earth is not your real home." His powerful stories forced people to think.

But teen Jesus, the future teacher, had still more to learn. He absorbed all the books of Hebrew Scripture, not only the Written Torah. He studied the Prophets and learned Jewish history in books like Joshua, Judges, Samuel, Kings, and Isaiah. He studied beautiful and powerful Jewish writings, like the Psalms, Proverbs, Job, Ecclesiastes, and the Song of Solomon.

When the lettering on a religious scroll became too worn to read, the scroll was placed in a synagogue storeroom called a *genizah* ("hiding place") and eventually buried in a cemetery. In this way, Jews preserved good writings, including any paper that contained God's Name.

Most of all, teen Jesus was keenly aware of Scripture prophecies regarding God's Chosen One, the Messiah, a king and shepherd (Micah 5:2–5) and a suffering servant (Isaiah 42 and 53). Rabbis linked the Messiah's coming to a time when God would rule the earth, a time they called the "Kingdom of Heaven." Jesus had a lot to think about.

Working and Going to School

Part of being a proper Jewish man in Jesus' culture was working to help support his family. Torah said work had dignity and was necessary for happiness. Again, Joseph exemplified the strong, good Jewish father. Many scholars believe Joseph taught teen Jesus his own trade (Mark 6:3) while Jesus privately continued rabbinical studies.

Jesus would need a second job, because Torah said a rabbi or synagogue teacher could not accept pay for teaching Scripture. As a good son, he would have supported himself and his mother after Joseph died. St. Paul followed the same rule. Though educated in the Law by a respected teacher, he worked as a tent maker (Acts 18:1–3).

The Greek word for Joseph's occupation is *tekton*, which means "artisan" or "skilled workman." A *tekton* may have worked in wood, metal, or stone. As a carpenter, Joseph would have made plows, yokes, cabinets, furniture, wheels, and doors for villagers—and taught Jesus to do the same.

Occupations in Jesus' time included teachers, farmers, shepherds, fabric and carpet weavers, field workers, fishermen, woodworkers, stone cutters, masons, sailors, sandal makers, pottery makers, fullers (dry cleaners), iron smiths, tanners, leather workers, goldsmiths, jewelers, millers, perfumers, bakers, oil-pressers, dyers, tailors, merchants, traders, tax collectors, tent makers, wine makers, and gravediggers.

Bargil Pixner cites an old story that indicates carpenters were well respected in Jewish society. A traveler came into a town seeking an answer to a vexing problem. He asked for a rabbi, but the town had none—so he asked for a carpenter. Pixner saw an implication: Carpenters knew the Law well and observed Torah faithfully.

Sepphoris and "Hypocrites"—A Link to Jesus?

During the years Jesus was growing up, Herod Antipas was rebuilding the ruins of Sepphoris, after the Romans burned it and sold its rebellious residents into slavery. Josephus later called Herod Antipas' new capital city "the ornament of Galilee."

Nazareth's artisans could easily see the construction site at Sepphoris, perched on a hill across the valley. In the DVD *An Archaeological Search for Jesus*, James Strange says it's possible Joseph and Jesus often packed their tools and walked to and from Sepphoris, an hour's journey each way, to find work.

In the Gospels, Jesus repeatedly used the unflattering word *hypocrite*, which is the Greek word for "actor." It's possible that Jesus learned

Photo Credit: Todd Bolen/BiblePlaces.com

Theater at Sepphoris, close to Nazareth. A second theater, found in Tiberias and built around 18 AD, means Jesus might have seen hypocrites or actors in his time.

it in Sepphoris, where Herod Antipas built a 4,000-seat Greek-style amphitheater. An amphitheater is built in a semicircular shape and lined with sloped rows of seats. This theater may have been built during Jesus' youth, though no one can say for sure.

However, archaeologists have also excavated an ampitheater near Tiberias, a Jewish city about eighteen miles from Nazareth. That theater has been dated to 20 AD, definitely within Jesus' day. Imagine Jesus' wonder if he had seen Greek actors or *hypocrites* perform a classic drama, complete with masks and chorus.

There's no doubt teen Jesus saw through the real hypocrites of his day, those who "do not practice what they teach," but "do all their deeds to be seen by others; for they make their phylacteries broad and their fringes long" (Matthew 23:3, 5). Such exaggerated shows of piety earned Jesus' disgust. A head phylactery, found at Qumran, was so small a postage stamp could cover it—showing that there were many humble worshippers, who felt no need to advertise their faith.

Preparing for a Tough Career

Teen Jesus trained hard for the difficult life of a rabbi. During the first century, many rabbis walked back and forth across the Holy Land, attracting followers/disciples. Dependent on people's hospitality for food and shelter, they faced hunger, thirst, loneliness, and extreme weather. They taught long hours in homes, synagogues, and outdoors—and often publicly debated one another. Jesus knew crowds would hound him, leaving him little time for sleep and "no leisure even to eat" (Mark 6:31).

He also knew he would confront prejudice. Jews in Judea's sophisticated capital of Jerusalem looked down on Galileans with their "guttural style of pronunciation"—and Jesus' accent would have been obvious during debates. But, cautions David Bivin, many Galilean rabbis were better educated in Scripture and were better trained in ethics than Judean rabbis.

After a Long Day of Work and Study, the Family Meal

Finally, at sunset, Jesus and Joseph's workday ended and they headed home, where the family washed their hands and gathered to share their main meal. Jewish families likely ate together, sitting on the floor or on the rooftop, weather permitting, around a large mat that Mary had set with food. As head of the family, Joseph gave thanks to God for bringing forth their food from the earth. Only after blessing God did he break and share bread with his family. Jews believed eating unblessed food was "stealing" from God.

A community pot or platter held the main course—either a savory stew of lentils, leeks, chickpeas, onions, and garlic, or a porridge dish of parched cracked wheat (something like couscous), seasoned with onions, cilantro, and cumin, and mixed with yogurt. Perhaps Mary also served one or more finger foods: dried apricots or raisins, *globi* (balls made of flour mixed with curd cheese, then fried and dipped in honey), cucumbers and greens from the garden, sweet cakes of pressed dates or figs mixed with spices and nuts, or pickled olives, onions, and citrons, a lemonlike fruit.

When Jesus fasted, he might have eaten pods from carob trees. The leathery pods, which ripened in summer, were fed to livestock; however, the poor ate them when food was scarce. The Prodigal Son in Luke 15:11–24 was hungry enough to eat them. Inside a mature brown pod, four to five inches long, nestle oval beans, each about the size of a baby aspirin. Ancient jewelers compared the size and weight of precious gems to one, two, or even three carob beans or *carats*, an Arabic word jewelers still use. Carob, which tastes a bit like cocoa, is used today to make the artificial chocolate in diabetic foods.

Since forks had not yet been invented, family members used pieces of freshly baked bread to scoop up the thick stew or porridge.

Many Middle Easterners still eat this way. The family might also have moistened their bread by dipping it in olive oil, vinegar, or yogurt that was thin enough to drink.

With their main meal in the evening, Jewish families often drank wine, which they believed helped digestion. But wine had other healthful uses. Its alcoholic content helped heal cuts cleanly when poured on open wounds; it also took the sting out of insect bites. People made wine from fermented grapes and sometimes added raisins, honey, fruit juice, water, or spices. Then, as now, good table manners meant not eating more than one's share or drinking too much wine, which the rabbis frowned upon.

After supper, the family prayed again. Rabbis believed that the blessing after a meal—motivated by gratitude, not hunger—was more important than the blessing before. They again washed their hands, likely by rinsing their fingertips twice as they poured water from a pitcher over a bowl to catch the excess water for other uses.

Photo Credit: Todd Bolen/BiblePlaces.com

Shepherding was a common occupation when Jesus lived. During warm months, a barrier of stones in front of a sheepfold protected the flock at night; shepherds guarded the entrance.

Some Pharisees, compulsive about ritual purity, washed all the way to their elbows.

Jewish villagers, who started their workday before dawn, went to bed early. Jesus and his family retired to an indoor sleeping area or, if the weather was warm and dry, climbed to their open-air rooftop. There, in the still darkness, they stood together and prayed the *Amidah* and the *Shema*. Guided by Torah, they had spent their day in the presence of the God they praised, thanked, and lovingly served. Now, caressed by a cool night breeze, they unrolled their straw sleeping mats and wrapped themselves in their warm cloaks. Lying down, they entrusted themselves to God's care and fell asleep under the starry heavens.

Questions for Discussion

1. Jesus didn't comment on, judge, or confront every political "hot-button" issue of his time; for example, slavery, which was a commonly accepted institution, though we now recognize it as a repugnant evil. But he DID say to treat all people, including those we don't like or get along with, with the same love and respect we have for ourselves. What issues today challenge us to live by Jesus' words?

2. In Matthew 23:1–7, Jesus speaks of hypocrites, people who live by the saying, "Do as I say, not as I do." Give examples of hypocritical behavior you've seen. What about "posers"? What makes a person hypocritical in our day? Think of some episodes of hypocrisy you have encountered. They may be from an institution or from an individual. What were they? (No names necessary!)

3. In Middle Eastern culture, one's honor, especially family honor, takes precedence over all else, even if it means lying to "save face." Sometimes people tell "white lies" to avoid hurting someone or to prevent a larger evil. Under what circumstances do you think it's okay to tell a white lie—or when not telling the whole truth might be considered necessary, or even good?

EIGHT

"R&R": Sabbath, Weddings, and Holidays

A man should always take care not to distress his wife, for women's tears are close to the heart of G-d.

—Talmud

Working hard without a break wears on the human spirit. Just as we look forward to weekends and holidays, Jewish families looked forward to the Sabbath, which began at sunset every Friday. Quiet settled over the land, as the people welcomed God's day of rest. All labor stopped. Families gathered and greeted one another with *"Shabbat Shalom,"* which means "peace of the Sabbath."

Inside their swept and tidied homes, fragrant with cinnamon, women lit the Sabbath lamp that burned until sunset on Saturday. (Jewish days last from sunset to sunset.) Families shared a cup of wine and blessed the children of the household with a beautiful prayer that begins, "The Lord bless you and keep you" (Numbers 6:24–26). So began twenty-four hours of prayer, rest, and Scripture study, both at home and in the synagogue.

The Mishna forbade thirty-nine works on the Sabbath. For example, men couldn't tie or untie a rope, write or erase two letters, or hammer one last blow. Women couldn't weave or sew two stitches, kindle a fire, or make bread. However, the Law said any Sabbath restriction could be broken to save a life. On Friday, Mary and the other women cooked and baked enough food to last for two days, allowing for family discussions of God's goodness and blessings while eating unheated, unhurried meals.

Besides the Sabbath, Jewish families enjoyed time off from work and household chores after attending synagogue services during the yearly religious holidays. Some of these festivals lasted for a week, something like our Christmas and Easter vacations. A wedding, too, meant a massive celebration. In Jesus' day, feasting, drinking, music, and dancing at weddings went on for a week—or longer.

One Big, Happy Family

Jewish girls usually married between the ages of fourteen and sixteen and boys, eighteen to twenty. By custom, the groom's parents chose his bride, since she linked the two families; however, he could choose a wife for himself. In biblical times, the groom's parents approached the bride's parents and discussed a "bride price," paid by the groom to the bride's father. They signed a wedding contract, a solemn prenuptial agreement as legally binding as marriage.

During the yearlong betrothal period, the groom built a dwelling, usually a one-room addition onto his father's house. Meanwhile, the bride—who left her father's house forever—made clothing for herself and prepared the household items she would need.

Just as we look forward to taking a break from school and work to celebrate our harvest at Thanksgiving, the Jews' favorite time for weddings was autumn, after the grape and olive crops were harvested and stored. The entire village attended a marriage celebration, along with the couple's extended family and friends from other villages.

The evening before the marriage, the triumphant groom and his jubilant male friends—shouting, singing, clapping, shaking tambourines, and playing flutes—wound their way through the village to the home of the bride's parents.

Freshly bathed, the bride and the groom had anointed their hair and clothing with perfume or scented oil. They both wore crowns or wreaths of flowers. Although ancient makeup containers have been discovered (dark kohl for eyes, red *sikra* for lips and cheeks, and reddish-gold henna for hands and nails), a Jewish bride was urged in song to be "clean as a doe." Ideally, her face shone with inner beauty.

She likely wore a dress she'd made herself and embroidered with her own designs, leather sandals with ankle straps, and jewelry like gold rings, earrings, bracelets, armlets, ankle bangles, and forehead rounds. With her long hair falling free but covered, and her radiant face veiled, she waited until the groom arrived and claimed her.

Then the joyful procession—with the bride riding a donkey or carried on a litter and surrounded by bridesmaids, who lit the way with oil lamps—headed back to the home of the groom's parents. There, all present blessed the couple. Games, music, and dancing followed, but the bride and her attendants modestly withdrew for the night.

One Big, Happy Party!

Next morning, the wedding took place outside, under a small tent or canopy called a *chuppah*, which means "to cover," as a husband shields his beloved from harm. In ancient times, Jewish parents planted a cedar tree when a baby boy was born and a pine tree when a girl was born. When they married, their canopy was made of branches woven from both trees.

The marriage contract, the groom's promise to support his wife, was read aloud. The groom gave his bride a gift—money, a gold ring, or jewelry—which symbolized her value and dedicated her to him.

After this simple ceremony, the long celebration began. Dressed in festive robes, likely borrowed, wedding guests feasted on roasted sheep or goat and drank fine wine. Sounds of laughter, clapping, dancing, tambourines, flutes, and ululations, the women's cries of joy, filled the air. John Pilch says Middle Eastern musicians repeated a basic pattern of notes: "all the white keys from E just above middle C to E an octave below." The intoxicating music, he adds, made "one continuous sound like . . . a siren."

A Jewish Orthodox wedding, with the bride and groom standing under a **chuppah** *(bridal tent or canopy).*

Hebrew men and women danced energetically, but in separate groups. Circling gracefully with the other young men, Jesus would have clapped his hands and pounded his feet to the music's fast, driving rhythm. Girls sang and danced in the vineyards, trying to catch the boys' attention.

Jews were not the only ancient people who entertained themselves with board games. Irving Finkel of the British Museum translated cuneiform (wedge-shaped symbols) instructions for how to play the "Royal Game of Ur," a board game that was popular 4,600 years ago. The ancient city of Ur was in Sumeria, a land the Greeks called Mesopotamia, now Iraq. Two players, using dice made from animal knucklebones, rolled numbers to race their five pieces around and off a game board made of twenty squares.

Boys also likely ran races, wrestled, and competed with slingshots. Love poems, riddles, jesters or "clowns" who sang humorous verses that teased the groom, and even Torah study were all part of Jewish weddings. Children spun *dreidels* (tops) and played ball, ring-toss, or hopscotch. Adults played board games that were similar to chess and threw dice. As the guests mingled, teens could observe one another and pick a potential mate.

Jesus and Marriage

Jesus enjoyed life and lived it to the fullest. He performed his first public miracle at a wedding. "The Son of Man came eating and drinking, and they say, 'Look, a glutton and a drunkard, a friend of tax collectors and sinners!'" (Matthew 11:19). Rabbis discouraged people from remaining single. They taught that marriage and children were vital to God's plan, man's good, and happiness. So, if Jesus chose not to marry, why not?

Because young rabbis often spent years away from home in study— and more years as traveling teachers—they sometimes waited to marry until they reached their late thirties or forties. One rabbi who lived after Jesus' time remained unmarried for life because, he said, he was in love with Torah. This means an unmarried Jewish rabbi in his early thirties, although uncommon, was not unheard of.

Moreover, wrote Todd Bolen, Jesus was deeply aware of his mission and knew he would die soon. Because of Jesus' charisma, teachings, and miracles, Bolen added, people might not have "held his unmarried status against him."

Capernaum

The Gospels hint at Jesus' respect for his apostles' marriages when he later chose Capernaum as his home base. Capernaum was a fishing village on the Sea of Galilee and home to the apostles Peter, Andrew, James, John, and Matthew. John, the youngest apostle and thought to be still in his mid-teens, was the only one not married.

According to the Mishna, a married man needed his wife's permission to study with a rabbi and be away from home longer than thirty days. It's likely that Jesus often returned to Capernaum so the apostles could spend time with and care for their families. Peter and Andrew (and any other brothers, single and married) all lived with their own families in their father Jonah's extended compound—which some archaeologists believe they have found—and that they offered Jesus (and maybe Mary) a room there, too.

When Jesus spoke of his followers "hating" their fathers, mothers, wives and children, says David Bivin, he used a Hebrew word that means to "love less" or "put in second place"—*not* to "disown" or "despise." Jesus simply put God's kingdom *first*.

Besides the weekly Sabbath and attending weddings, teen Jesus and his family looked forward to celebrating the major holidays. Like ours, Jewish feasts/festivals still occur throughout the year—some in autumn, some in spring, and one in winter. The three fall festivals, like weddings, occurred after the hard work of harvesting was finished.

Autumn Holidays: Tabernacles, Trumpets, and Day of Atonement

During the eight-day feast of *Sukkoth* (Tabernacles or Booths), Jews rejoiced over the grape and olive harvest. Jesus' family joined others putting up tents (tabernacles) or building "booths," huts made of

Putting grapes into a winepress for crushing during the fall harvest; weddings often followed.

branches, and living outdoors for a week. This recalled their ancestors' forty years in the desert after Moses led them out of Egypt.

In Jerusalem, the high priest poured a water-offering onto the altar. Acrobats and jugglers performed at night in the **Women's Court**, lit by four giant branched candlesticks so tall that priests used ladders to trim their wicks. From the balcony, women watched the men below, who were holding torches and dancing. On the last day, pilgrims waved palms, carried citrons, and processed around the altar with singing and music.

Jesus celebrated the New Year, but not in January. *Rosh Hoshana* (Trumpets) fell in autumn. Long blasts of a *shofar* (a ram's-horn trumpet) announced the start of the Jewish New Year, when God examined deeds in his "books." At home and synagogue, families reflected on their actions, repaired past mistakes, and made New Year's resolutions to bring God's blessings on them. The lunar-based Hebrew calendar begins with the creation of Adam and Eve.

"R&R"

So what year is it for the Jewish people? The year 5774 begins in September 2013.

Trumpet blasts also began *Yom Kippur*, the solemn Day of Atonement and the Jews' holiest day. The high priest laid the people's sins on the forehead of a "scapegoat" that was then driven into the desert. On this day of repentance, Jesus and his family attended synagogue, asked forgiveness from God and others for their offenses, and observed the "great fast," which meant no eating or drinking from sunset (the day before) until three stars appeared that evening.

Spring Holidays: Passover, Pentecost, and Lots

Springtime also had three feasts, including the biggest of all for Jewish families, Passover and Unleavened Bread.

Passover, the first and greatest feast, will be covered in detail in chapter 9. It is followed by *Shavuot* (Weeks), also called Pentecost or First Fruits, which had its roots on the second day of Passover, when Temple priests cut barley sheaves to mark the beginning of the grain harvest. The feast of Pentecost (Greek for "fiftieth day") took place fifty days later, when the priests offered "first fruits"—two large loaves of bread made of the finest new wheat. In Nazareth and other villages, farmers offered the first fruits of their crops. In our part of the world, wheat is harvested in the fall. However, Christians celebrate Pentecost, the coming of the Holy Spirit, fifty days after Easter.

The third Spring holiday, **Purim** (Lots), recalled Queen Esther, who'd married a Persian king. His advisor, Haman, had drawn "lots" to determine the day he would hang Esther's uncle Mordecai and other Jews who refused to bow down to him. Neither the king nor Haman knew Esther was Jewish, until she revealed it during a banquet for her husband. Enraged by Haman's plot against the innocent, the king embraced Esther and her people and hung Haman on the gallows built for Mordecai. During Purim, Jesus' family celebrated the ways God constantly brings unexpected success through "hidden miracles." Jewish congregations still boo, hiss, and sound noisemakers when Haman's name is read in the synagogue—a reminder that silence in the face of evil is wrong.

The Winter Holiday: Hanukkah

Celebrated around November/December, *Hanukkah* (Hebrew for "Dedication"), or the festival of Lights, recalled the time when the Seleucid king of Syria outlawed Sabbath observance, kosher laws and circumcision, and sacrificed pigs in the First Temple. Outraged, the Jewish Maccabees led a long rebellion. Finally victorious in 164 BC, they purified and re-dedicated the Temple to God. The people believed the *menorah* (a seven-branched golden candlestick that symbolized God's Presence) burned miraculously without oil during the eight days required to consecrate the altar. During *Hanukkah*, you might see lit *menorahs* mingling with Christmas lights.

Questions for Discussion

1. In Jesus' time, it was common for girls as young as twelve and boys as young as thirteen to marry. In some cultures, families still marry off "child brides." They might want to gain favor with a wealthy relative within their clan or forge a political alliance with another clan. What if your family made such an important decision for you? Can you imagine being given in marriage to someone you've never met? What would that be like? How would you handle it?

2. A classic movie, *Fiddler on the Roof,* depicts an old Jewish custom of families asking a matchmaker to find suitable mates for their children. If a child balked and married someone he or she loved, they could be ostracized by their family. How would you react to an arranged marriage? Would you sacrifice the love of your family for the love you choose? And for something no one in biblical times ever heard of, there's online dating. What are the pros and cons of finding a girlfriend or boyfriend online?

NINE

Passover, Pilgrimage, and the Second Temple

I was glad when they said to me, "Let us go to the house of the Lord!" Our feet are standing within your gates, O Jerusalem.

—Psalm 122:1

The glorious Jewish feast of Passover, and the next day's Feast of Unleavened Bread, commemorated Moses leading the people out of Egypt. At the **Seder** (Passover meal), children learned the story of their ancestors' Exodus from Egypt, how Pharaoh refused to let them go, even after nine terrible plagues. But *Yahweh* saved the Jewish families from the tenth plague—the death of every household's firstborn child and animal when the angel of death *passed over*—because they smeared their doorposts with blood from a slaughtered lamb.

Ideally, Jews were urged to travel to Jerusalem for three annual feasts: Passover (in the Jewish month that corresponds to April), Pentecost (June), and Tabernacles (around September/October). But many Hebrews, wrote Rabbi Shmuel Safrai, might have journeyed to Jerusalem only once a year, or "once every few years or perhaps only once in a lifetime"—choosing, instead, to celebrate religious holidays at home.

However, the festival of choice for a pilgrimage was definitely Passover, the most celebrated Jewish holiday. Observed in the spring, it often coincides with Easter. According to Luke (2:41), "Every year his parents went to Jerusalem for the festival of the Passover." Of course, Jesus went, too.

> Christians, Jews, and Muslims all claim Jerusalem as their Holy City. For Christians, Jerusalem is tied to Jesus. Jews, with historic roots in the region, connect as a people there. Two Islamic mosques now occupy the site of the Second Temple. Inside one, the Dome of the Rock, visitors can see the top of Mount Moriah, where the Prophet Muhammad, descended from Abraham's first son, Ishmael, stood before ascending to heaven. Muslims honor Abraham as their father, and Moses and Jesus as prophets. Jews believe Abraham's second son, Isaac, was their ancestor. From Jesus' Jewish roots came Christianity. Thus, Abraham is called the "father of three faiths," all of which believe in only one God.

On the Road to Jerusalem

During Passover's weeklong celebration, Jerusalem's population might have swelled by 20,000 to 30,000. Estimates of the exact number vary greatly. Long processions of pilgrims, who sang psalms as they walked or rode donkeys, packed the roads to Judea's capital. Jews from distant North Africa, Greece, and beyond arrived at port cities by boat and merged with crowds on foot. The defiant and unruly among them increased the risk of riots, so Romans kept a close eye on the pilgrims. Jesus surely saw grim military patrols marching toward the holy city.

To avoid robbers who preyed on isolated travelers, small bands of pilgrims joined traders' caravans—long lines of linked camels loaded with silk, cinnamon, incense, nard, and news from the East. Travel was never easy. Rain turned dirt roads to mud. Hot, dry weather brought clouds of dust and flies. Road-weary pilgrims had to dodge Roman cavalry on horseback, as well as bumps, potholes, and deep

Western Wall prayer area, filled with holiday worshippers.

ruts cut by chariot wheels. Everyone pushed to cover as many miles as possible before daylight faded.

As night fell, weary travelers stopped for shelter at an inn or way station, where they ate and rested in safety. A typical inn was likely a two-story structure, built around a square courtyard with a well. Families would have slept crowded together upstairs on floor mats, while pack animals were fed, watered, and stabled on the ground level. Early the next morning, people were back on the crowded roads.

Excitement grew with each passing day until Jerusalem came into view, perched in majesty on the purple ridge of the Judean Mountains. From a distance, wrote Josephus, the chalk-white Temple sparkled like snow on Mount Moriah. Pilgrims might have kissed their sacred ground as they entered the Holy City. There, their history came to life. There they connected to their father, Abraham, who had once visited Melchizedek, king and high priest of Salem, as Jerusalem was once called.

Archaeologists have unearthed remnants of Jerusalem's splendor that Jesus saw: massive gates, walls fortified with towers, the Antonia

Passover, Pilgrimage, and the Second Temple

Pool of Siloam excavations, where Jesus cured the man born blind (John 9:1–12).

Photo Credit: Todd Bolen/BiblePlaces.com

Fortress, the Hasmonean palace, stone archways, shops, a theater, a sports arena for chariot races, and a vast underground sewer system. Above its well-engineered tunnel, a stepped road paved in carved stones climbed nearly 2,000 feet from the huge Pool of Siloam to the Temple that crowned Mount Moriah, high above the city. There, said Jewish tradition, Abraham had once led Isaac to be sacrificed.

King Herod the Great's Second Temple

A towering retaining wall enclosed the Temple complex, built on an immense manmade platform. Double the size of Solomon's First Temple, Herod's Temple could have held about thirty football fields. The Second Temple was built of squared stones, or ashlars, so perfectly cut they fit together without mortar. Polished to resemble glistening white marble, the massive limestone blocks weighed from five to seventy tons each.

As Torah prescribed, the priests offered a sacrifice to God every morning and late afternoon—not just on Passover. To take part in the daily worship ritual, Jesus and his family rose before dawn, bathed in a *mikveh*, and climbed one of many stairways that led up from the streets to the Temple Mount. They joined the countless other pilgrims who streamed toward one of seven gates leading into the outermost **Court of the Gentiles**.

Money and Moneychangers: Necessary Evils for Pilgrims

Money in Jesus' world took the form of coins. The silver coins minted in Greece, Rome, Egypt, and Persia bore engraved images of rulers, animals, and pagan gods. Torah forbade reproducing the image of a man, animal, or bird, so Jewish coins (*shekels, talents*) bore writing, symbols like a seven-branched candlestick, flowers, and/or fruit. Though the word *shekel* means "weight" in Hebrew, we don't know its exact weight. What is known is that 3,000 *shekels* made one *talent*, which was heavy.

Families brought their own Passover lamb from home or bought one in Jerusalem. Vendors likely sold sacrificial animals near the gates of the Court of the Gentiles. Temple moneychangers had tables nearby. Every Jewish male, twenty or older, had to pay a yearly tax of half a silver shekel to support the Temple (Exodus 30:13–14). To pay the tax—and buy food, lodging, and a lamb—pilgrims from foreign lands exchanged their "idolatrous" money for Hebrew coins of equal value. Moneychangers often shortchanged them.

Entering the Temple: First Stop, the Court of the Gentiles

In their beautifully illustrated book *Secrets of Jerusalem's Temple Mount*, Leen and Kathleen Ritmeyer give us an idea of the magnificence of the Second Temple, with vivid descriptions of its courts, arches, porches, gates, and chambers.

Inside the vast Court of the Gentiles, immense covered porches, supported by gigantic decorated pillars or columns, ran along all four of its sides. The most splendid of these long, open hallways was called the Royal Stoa. During the day, people socialized under the walkways' shade and listened to rabbis teach.

Here, Temple authorities posted death warnings in Greek and Latin against Gentiles, or non-Jews, going further. Here, too, was the stopping point for any Hebrew who was ritually impure. This included women after childbirth, who were barred from entering until they had offered a sacrifice. According to Luke (2:24), Mary offered a sacrifice of two pigeons.

The Women's Court: Where Mary Worshipped

Each Court was built higher than the one before. So, along with other "pure" men and women, Jesus' family surged up more stairs and through more gates, overlaid with gold and silver, into the Women's Court. This Court had a raised gallery on three sides, benches for public assemblies of men and women, the Temple treasury with thirteen horn-shaped boxes marked for different donations, and four large "Chambers." Today, we're not familiar with huge chambers inside a church, set apart for different purposes and activities, but the Second Temple was expansive enough to accommodate them.

Nazarites, separated from the community by vow, used one chamber. Torah speaks of these men and women who vowed to live apart, consecrated to God's service, for a short time or for life (Numbers 6). During that specific period, they did not drink wine, cut their hair, or touch dead bodies. In the Temple's Chamber of the Nazarites, they took their vows—or ended their vows and cut their hair.

In another chamber, healed lepers presented themselves to be examined by a priest and ritually cleansed before they could rejoin the community. Wine and grain offerings, olive oil, firewood, and musical instruments were stored in the last two. Throughout the Temple, other smaller chambers were dedicated to activities like salting meat offerings or baking bread. The Sanhedrin met daily in the Chamber of Hewn Stone, where rabbis and their disciples sat and studied Torah.

Mary usually stayed in the Women's Court to worship. However, according to the Mishna, women were required to bring sacrifices and offerings and, like men, could enter the **Priests' Court** with animals and food and carry them to the altar.

The Men's Court or Court of Israel

Jesus and thousands of other men climbed still higher, up fifteen semicircular steps to the massive, bronze-plated Nicanor Gate. There, worshippers waited for sunrise, when the morning rite of sacrifice to *Yahweh* would begin. On signal, the gate swung open with a deafening clang. The huge assembly poured into the **Men's Court**. All stood, looking up at the altar, hushed and ready to share in their worship ceremony.

The Priests' Court: A Holy Place of Sacrifice

Above the assembly, a gigantic stone altar of sacrifice stood in the center of the Priests' Court. Nearby, one or more unblemished rams, oxen, or lambs were secured by one of twenty-four head rings fixed to the ground. Each animal's life would be offered to God in place of the people, for forgiveness of sins, thanksgiving, or to restore ritual purity. A priest washed his hands and feet in a huge copper basin before sacrificing the people's offerings, including pigeons and doves.

While some priests removed fat and cut up the washed and salted meat on marble tables, others carried choice portions to a ramp leading upward, where a fire blazed on top of the mammoth altar. In preparation for the burnt-offering ritual, priests recited the Ten Commandments, prayed the *Shema*, and poured the animals' sacrificial blood on the altar's four "horns," or peaks. The blood drained down a gutter into the Kidron Valley.

Meanwhile, yet another priest, chosen by lot for the honor, burned incense on a golden altar inside the priests' private sanctuary, called the House of God. When he finished, all the priests gathered on their Court's wide stairs. Standing under a huge Golden Vine before the veiled door of their holiest place, they lifted their hands in blessing over the vast assembly of God's people.

Finally, the priests placed all the offerings in the altar fire. Meat, grain, wine, and baked cakes of finest flour were consumed in the leaping flames, offerings for *Yahweh* alone. Sweet-smelling incense masked the odors of blood, scorched meat, and burnt bread. Like the people's prayers, its thick white clouds rose heavenward.

As the offerings burned, a choir of **Levites** sang joyous psalms. Levite musicians accompanied the choir with ceremonial instruments: flutes, lyres, harps, trumpets, and cymbals. At times, the people joined in. Thousands of early morning worshippers, all on their feet with their hands held high, praised God's goodness in one thundering voice. Music rocked the Temple. The Mishna said the Levites' flutes and cymbals could be heard in Jericho, seventeen miles away. What powerful energy Jesus must have felt! Later that day, Jewish families gathered again for the afternoon sacrifice.

The House of God and the Holy of Holies

During worship, Jesus must have gazed in awe at the House of God, a towering building that stood at one end of the Priests' Court, above the broad stairs. Hidden from view by a veil of exquisite beauty, this sacred space held many Temple treasures, including the gold-covered incense altar, a gold table for showbread (bread of the Lord), and the always-lit, seven-branched golden candlestick that symbolized God's constant Presence. The House of God's highest and innermost sanctuary, the veiled and golden-walled **Holy of Holies**, stood empty.

Once this most sacred space for the Jewish people had housed the Ark of the Covenant—an acacia wood chest, covered in gold, with rings and poles for carrying. But the Ark had been lost, likely when

Solomon's First Temple was destroyed. Inside had been the stone tablets inscribed with Moses' Ten Commandments, a dish of manna, and Aaron's rod that had blossomed. Its sculpted gold cover, called the Mercy Seat, portrayed two angels with outstretched wings. On the yearly Day of Atonement, the high priest entered the Holy of Holies alone to burn incense and pray.

Is anything left of the Jerusalem Jesus knew? The largest of three towers from Herod's palace is still visible. Astonished at the towers' height and immense building blocks, Titus spared them during his conquest. Devout Jews still gather to pray at the Western or Wailing Wall—a remnant of the retaining wall Herod the Great constructed around the Temple.

Celebration and Relaxation

Twice-daily sacrifice, prayer, public Torah reading, and hearing rabbis teach kept pilgrims within the Temple's Courts much of their time. Cheerful and relaxed, they enjoyed their leisure and stayed close to their traveling group—family and friends from Nazareth and nearby villages. Psalm 48:12–14 advised visitors: "Walk about Zion, go all around it, count its towers, consider well its ramparts; go through its citadels, that you may tell the next generation that this is God." The towers must have been impressive.

Josephus wrote that a priest blew a trumpet call across the city at the beginning and end of every Sabbath. Archaeologists found an eight-ton stone, inscribed "Belonging to the Place of Trumpeting," which likely fell from a Temple tower when it collapsed in 70 AD. Josephus also tells us that the Temple roof had spikes to keep birds from nesting on it.

Where did Jesus and his family spend the night? Some Passover pilgrims probably stayed in Jerusalem's private homes or in nearby villages, like Bethany. Many others camped in "tent cities," set up in two surrounding valleys, the Kidron and the Hinnom.

Not everything was perfect for pilgrims to Jerusalem. Herod the Great had infuriated his subjects by hanging a golden eagle, symbol of Rome, above a Temple gate. Roman soldiers mocked the Jewish congregations from the high walls of their adjoining barracks, the Antonia Fortress, where they peered down on the surging crowds.

Still, Jews connected to God and their heritage in the Temple. There they came together, a people united to worship by sacrifice. There they felt "whole," writes Karen Armstrong, "momentarily healed" from the pain of separation from God. "A day in your courts is better than a thousand elsewhere" (Psalm 84:10).

Temple Priests/Sadducees

Members of the priestly class descended from Moses' brother, Aaron, and belonged to the tribe of Levi. Written Torah (Leviticus 21:16–24) required them to be without blemish; that is, close to physical perfection. Chosen by the Sanhedrin and divided into twenty-four groups, they rotated Temple duty for two weeks a year.

Caretakers and cleaners of the Temple and its furnishings, priests changed the sacred bread loaves, trimmed candlewicks, and swept up sacrificial ashes from the altar. The Mishna says priests were lowered in baskets from the top of the Holy of Holies to polish its high walls, overlaid in gold plates. Levites, other descendants of Levi not chosen for the priesthood, also rotated duty as the priests' servant helpers.

Priests wore a linen tunic, puffy pants, a sash, and a turban. They shared in food and money offerings, and ate sacrificial meals. Josephus said the high priest dressed in priceless sacred vestments on the Day of Atonement: a *tekhelet* robe embellished with gold bells and pomegranates hanging from the hem, an embroidered sash, a gold-embroidered breastplate inlaid with jewels and precious stones engraved with the names of Israel's twelve tribes, a linen headdress or miter, and a gold crown engraved with the letters *YHWH*. A unique, ½-inch-diameter gold bell, discovered in Jerusalem's ancient sewer system, likely came from a priest's robe. The tiny bell still tinkled.

One apocryphal story says Mary grew up in the Temple, dedicated to its service. She was chosen by lot to spin the "true purple" in the Temple's veil, or curtain. Josephus said an "image of the universe" was seen in its colors: scarlet for fire, flax for earth, blue for air, and purple for the sea. The Mishna says it was embroidered with lions and eagles, and its massive size and thickness required 300 priests to wash it.

Passover Lambs

Based on the Hebrew/Babylonian lunar calendar, Passover always coincided with the full moon. The day before the feast, priests slaughtered thousands of lambs brought forward in the Temple, offered their blood on the altar as atonement, and returned each to the family who had presented it for their Seder meal that night. John the Baptist called Jesus the "Lamb of God," as he would die for his people during Passover (John 1:29).

> During a modern Passover Seder, Jews praise God, sing, drink four cups of wine, and eat prescribed foods. No one is sure if all this was part of the Passover meal in Jesus' day. Today's Seder dishes include *pesach* (Paschal/Passover lamb, usually a lamb shank), *matzot* (crackerlike, unleavened flatbread), *maror* (bitter herbs, like chicory and radishes), *karpas* (a spring vegetable, like parsley), a boiled egg, and *haroset* (a spread made of chopped dates, apples, almonds or walnuts mixed with cinnamon and wine).

Each Passover lamb was skewered on moist branches of pomegranate wood and roasted in a clay oven. Preparations took a long time, so families probably didn't eat the Passover meal until after dark, when the full moon was rising. Under its radiant light and by the soft glow of oil lamps, Jesus' family—as well as other Jews in Jerusalem, throughout the Holy Land, and scattered throughout the then-known world—gathered to celebrate God's saving goodness to his people.

Questions for Discussion

1. What holidays does your family celebrate in a big way? What ethnic traditions from your cultural heritage form a part of your celebration that your friends may not share or understand? What custom or tradition makes one holiday stand out from all the rest? (Hint: It doesn't have to be something that makes you happy. It could be something you find embarrassing or something you just don't like at all.)

2. You have probably travelled long distances, certainly distances greater than Jesus traveled when his only mode of transportation was his feet. Did you drive, fly, or take a train or boat? How did you prepare? What did you pack? What did you eat along the way?

3. What makes you like (or dislike) traveling a hundred miles or more from your home?

TEN

One Death,
Two Burials

*Like vinegar on a wound . . . Like a moth in clothing
or a worm in wood, sorrow gnaws at the human heart.*
—Proverbs 25:20

At some unknown time, Joseph's life faded and was gone. One ancient tradition, the "Story of Joseph the Carpenter," says he died around 18–19 AD, when Jesus would have been in his twenties. Torah says that, at Joseph's death, a close relative likely closed his eyes, "wept over him and kissed him" farewell (Genesis 50:1). The Jewish custom of respect for the dead—plus the Holy Land's warm climate—required proper burial as soon as possible. Ideally, this meant before sunset on the day of death; however, no burials were allowed on the Sabbath. What did a proper burial involve?

When Joseph died, Jesus and other grieving relatives would have washed and anointed his body with scented oil and perfumes (perhaps nard, myrrh, and aloeswood). Then, according to custom, they would have lovingly wrapped him in handmade strips of white linen or in a shroud/burial cloth, spread with spices. From the instant of his death until his burial that same day, Joseph's body was never left alone.

Preparing a corpse for burial—considered a highly virtuous act because the dead couldn't return the favor—made the family, house, furnishings, and everyone in it ritually unclean for seven days (Numbers 19:16–19). Here again, purity for a devout Jew was related to hygiene and to what one touched. Since food couldn't be prepared in the house until it (and everyone and everything in it) was cleansed by sprinkling with water, friends cared for the family's needs during the week of mourning that followed a burial. Jesus would not have participated in any religious rituals before having totally immersed himself in a *mikveh* and washed his clothes on the seventh day of his unclean state.

Family Burial Caves

Burials were always outside the town limits. Archaeologists describe a typical tomb of Jesus' day as either a naturally formed limestone cave, or a burial chamber carved out of nearby slopes. Steps led down into a square pit, dug out of the floor just inside the cramped entrance. This area was deep enough to allow family members' heads to clear the low ceiling as they stood to pray. The rock floor on the tomb's other three sides was left intact, forming waist-high benches to accommodate multiple burials. Some benches had headrests carved into the stone.

Archaeologists have also found burial grounds that resemble our cemeteries, including one at Qumran, where the Dead Sea Scrolls were discovered. When people died far from home or were too poor to afford a rock-hewn tomb, they were buried at the bottom of individual trench graves or shafts, dug five to seven feet deep. The corpse was laid flat and covered over with mud bricks. In this primary or basic burial, often in a "potter's field," or ground reserved for strangers and the penniless, the body was never moved.

We can't be certain how Joseph was laid to rest. However, burial in a family cave was an ancient and common Jewish practice in Jesus' time. By custom, Mary and other women relatives would have led the funeral procession to his gravesite, with Jesus and other male relatives carrying the corpse on an open litter.

Funerals and Visiting the Dead

Flute players and public lamentation were a necessary part of an honorable Jewish burial. Hired professional mourners cried, wailed, and threw dust into their hair as they walked barefoot in the procession. Family members fasted and tore their garments to symbolize their grief-torn hearts. If the usual custom was followed, Jesus' family placed Joseph's body inside a multiple burial cave, covered him with fragrant herbs, and placed small vials of perfume around the area—a necessary touch, since relatives visited the dead to pray during the required seven days of mourning.

The family then sealed their cave to deter grave robbers and animals, and to hold impurities inside. Weighing several hundred pounds, the rock seal was either a square boulder or a flat rounded stone that rolled, wheel-like, across a fitted groove at the cave entrance. During the return home, the funeral procession stopped seven times to mourn.

Life after Death . . . and Resurrection

Early Jews thought the shadowy spirits of the dead descended to a dark abyss, the underworld of *Sheol*, where there was neither reward nor punishment. However, in Luke 16 (19–31), Jesus said Lazarus was "carried away by the angels to be with Abraham," which indicates a place of reward in the afterlife.

Jesus also used the word *Gehenna* or *Gehinnom* (Matthew 5:29), often translated as "hell." However, the Jewish meaning was more like purgatory, where souls are purified for a period of time, rather than punished for eternity. The name was thought to have come from the Hinnom Valley outside Jerusalem's walls, once a pagan site used for child sacrifice.

The Jewish people believe that death is a "transition from one life to another," says Rabbi Aaron Parry. Early in the death journey, a soul might suffer by remaining attached to its body—until it sees it decay. Or, forgetting its earthly name, a soul may wander aimlessly when angels call it to the next world. One angel, Dumah, helps souls remember by asking them their names.

According to Jewish tradition, most departed souls suffer immense sadness and anguish because of their misdeeds, which separate them from God. Eventually, this pain makes them pure enough to see God and experience perfect joy. Some early rabbis believed reincarnation was a way for souls to make amends for past wrongs.

According to traditional Jewish belief, a soul "hovered" for three days after death, trying to reenter its body. However, by the fourth day, the corpse's appearance would have changed so much that the spirit no longer recognized itself and left. This belief adds to the awe of Lazarus' family when Jesus raised him from the dead after four days (John 11:1–44).

The Jewish belief in resurrection is rooted in Scripture: "Your dead shall live, their corpses shall rise" (Isaiah 26:19) and "many of those who sleep in the dust of the earth shall awake . . ." (Daniel 12:2).

Loculi, Arcosolia, Secondary Burials, and Bone Boxes

When families needed to make room for more bodies, they dug out more of their burial cave, cutting a fingerlike array of narrow perpendicular niches, or *loculi* (Latin plural), into the soft limestone walls. Each *loculus* (singular) looked like a ground-level tunnel—about two feet wide and two feet high, and five to six feet deep. When people peered inside the low opening to glimpse their loved one, they saw only blackness.

Instead of using simple dark shafts for their dead, some wealthy Jerusalem families owned large burial caves with an inner chamber that had artistically carved recesses, called *arcosolia*. Facing an *arcoso-*

Loculi *and* **arcosolium** *used for Jewish burials; these were found in the Hinnom Valley, outside Jerusalem.*

lium (singular), mourners saw their relative's corpse lying lengthwise on an open shallow shelf, beneath a gently rounded arch.

After a year inside a limestone cave's walls, the deceased's flesh, which was thought to be the source of sin, dried and fell off the bones. In Jesus' time, relatives then reentered the tomb and conducted a secondary burial. Most families collected the bones, which they believed still held the presence of the dead, and either piled them on the floor or reburied them in a pit covered with a stone slab.

Wealthy families, however, placed the bones of four to six adults, as well as the bones of several children and babies, in a stone ornamental burial box called an **ossuary**. Ossuaries or bone boxes—oblong chests with flat, round, or vaulted lids—were long enough to hold an adult's femur (the longest human bone), wide enough to hold a pelvis, and deep enough to hold a rib cage, says Craig Evans.

Ossuaries discovered beneath a Jerusalem chapel named **Dominus Flevit,** *Latin for "the Lord wept" (Luke 19:41).*

The names of the deceased were inscribed on the outside of the ossuary, which was then placed inside one of the tomb's *loculi*. This Jewish practice of secondary burial began around the time of Jesus' birth and lasted until roughly 70 AD.

Ossuaries in the News

A number of ancient ossuaries have been discovered, most in the twentieth century. Their contents have been both fascinating and controversial.

In 1941, an ossuary inscribed "Alexander (son) of Simon" was discovered inside a burial cave, along with pottery dated to the first century AD. Although "Simon" was a common Jewish name, "Alexander" was likely more typical in the Roman province of Cyrene, today's Libya. It has been suggested that this ossuary could be linked to Simon of Cyrene, the Passover pilgrim who helped Jesus carry his cross.

In 1990, archaeologists excavated what many believe was the family tomb of Caiaphas, the high priest who'd plotted Jesus' death (John 11:49), and found what could be his ossuary. Decorated with whorls of rosettes, the bone box inscribed with the name "Caiaphas" contained six skeletons. A coin, found inside a skull in the same burial cave, was imprinted "minted by Herod Agrippa." Agrippa ruled from 37–44 AD, not long after Jesus' death.

In 2002, the existence of the 2,000-year-old James Ossuary was announced. One of the most tantalizing and intriguing discoveries of our time, its exact origin is unknown and its authenticity is still subject to debate. The ossuary is inscribed in Aramaic: "James, son of Joseph, brother of Jesus." Some believe the inscription was forged. Others believe that the unbroken patina (a thin surface covering, due to age) in the engraved letters shows they are genuine. After a seven-year trial that began in 2005, a Jerusalem judge declared two antiquities dealers, who had been arrested and charged with forgery, not guilty. The judge cited insufficient evidence to prove wrongdoing. However, his verdict doesn't prove or disprove authenticity.

Cruel Justice

Jesus lived in a time and place of extremely cruel public executions—be it crucifixion by the Romans or stoning by the Jews. Over forty years ago, an archaeologist excavated evidence from an ossuary of the only known crucifixion victim to date. The man was in his twenties and had obviously come from a wealthy Jewish family. What the archaeologist discovered—inside one of eight ossuaries found in a family tomb near Jerusalem—was a right heel bone, penetrated by a 4.5-inch-long iron nail. The man's name, Yehohanan, was scratched on the outside of the ossuary.

What caused a crucifixion victim's death? Medical experts aren't certain; their theories range from asphyxia (inability to breathe) to heart failure due to shock, caused by severe trauma, blood and fluid loss, exhaustion, and extreme pain. One thing is certain—crucifixion was a terrible and violent death.

Pontius Pilate, prefect of Judea, lived in a palace in the port city of Caesarea Maritima, built by Herod the Great. There, archaeologists found a stone plaque inscribed with his name and title. During the Jewish festivals, a time ripe for riots, Pilate and his troops traveled to Jerusalem. Josephus wrote of his cruelty and said he took money from the Temple treasury to help pay for Jerusalem's aqueduct. Pilate's high-ranking protector in Rome, Sejanus, had been executed in 31 AD for plotting against Emperor Tiberias. Fear of being suspected of disloyalty likely influenced Pilate's decision to crucify Jesus, a leader the people wanted to make king, and so keep order during Passover.

Is the Shroud of Turin Authentic?
You Decide . . .

John 20:5 refers to the "linen wrappings" used in Jesus' burial. The Shroud of Turin is a linen burial cloth, woven in a herringbone pattern, which some believe was Jesus' shroud. It's named for the city in Italy where it's been stored since the Middle Ages.

The Shroud measures about 14 feet by 3½ feet and is stained with human blood (male, type AB). Its negative photographic image shows a crucified man around 5'11" tall and weighing 170 pounds. He has long, parted hair and a beard. Nail wounds appear between his wrist bones. His head shows marks from thorns and his body has marks from a whip. Pollen and flowers found on the Shroud are from plants that grew in Jerusalem.

In 1988, three laboratories—one in Oxford, one in Zurich, and one in Tucson—conducted carbon dating tests on pieces of its fabric. These scientists concluded the Shroud was painted, a clever "medieval fake." But others believe the lab results were distorted. You can find more information at http://www.shroudofturin4journalists.com.

The Shroud may not prove to be evidence of Jesus' crucifixion, but the historian Josephus wrote about the event. Among his writings

Replica of a Latin stone inscription, found in Caesarea Maritima in 1962, which says "Pontius Pilate, Prefect of Judea."

is a paragraph about Jesus, though early Christians might have tried to enhance it. Paul Maier projects Josephus' original wording: Jesus was a good and wise man, who had many disciples; Pontius Pilate condemned him to die by crucifixion; Jesus' disciples said he appeared, alive, to them three days later; Jesus might have been the prophesied Messiah; and his "tribe of the Christians" had not disappeared.

Questions for Discussion

1. In Jesus' day, death touched just about everyone for all of their lives. If you reached your teen years in his time, it is very likely that one or more of your brothers and sisters would not have survived childhood. Have you ever been to a funeral or seen one on TV or in the movies? What ethnic customs were observed? Some people may want their funeral to be a celebration of their lives. Others may want "weeping and gnashing of teeth." Which one would you opt for?

2. It is rare these days in the United States for families to play a role in the preparation of their loved ones for burial. We have seen how different it was in Jesus' time. How do you think it would feel to visit dead relatives up close, inside a dark burial cave, and then help remove their bones after a year?

3. There are many beliefs about life after death—heaven or hell, reincarnation, karma. How do you picture the afterlife? How is it like, or not like, what you have learned in religion classes?

Epilogue

G-d decides what shall befall a man, but not whether he shall be righteous or wicked.

—Talmud

So, what *did* Jesus do all day? He prayed and studied, ate and slept, worked and rested, lived among good people and bad—just as we do. He was an ordinary teen who grew up in an ordinary way, grounded in the culture of his day. The same questions haunted him that haunt other teens: "Who am I?" "Where did I come from?" "Why am I here?" The answers to those questions took a long time to answer, as they do for all of us. It has been said that Jesus' full awareness of who he was burst upon him at his adult baptism, when God said, "You are my Son, the Beloved" (Mark 1:11).

As a boy foreshadows the man he'll be, teen Jesus must have been a true friend. He never tried to impress the rich or powerful. He didn't play games to achieve social status, power, wealth, or praise. His best friends were simple, work-hardened men. But years of hard work and training made Jesus physically tough, too. Imagine Peter's awe when Jesus lifted him from the waves with one hand (Matthew 14:31).

Time passed for Jesus, as it does for us, connected by life's milestones. Along the way, he grew "in wisdom and in years" (Luke 2:52), becoming the focused, charismatic young man who would survive forty days alone in the wilderness, sleep soundly on a boat tossed by a raging storm, and bear excruciating pain with patience and dignity. One day, his mother watched him walk toward the horizon until he disappeared from view.

Healer, Teacher, Friend

When Jesus left home to begin his ministry of healing and teaching, he carried Hebrew Scripture in his heart, including the book of Isaiah—the same prophetic words copied on so many of the Qumran Scrolls. "Then the eyes of the blind shall be opened, and the ears of the deaf unstopped; then the lame shall leap like a deer, and the tongue of the speechless sing for joy" (Isaiah 35:5–6).

In their time, the Jewish people had seen many prophets and miracle-workers, teachers and healers. They recognized those who truly radiated *Shekinah*, the Divine Presence of God, as Jesus did. He was real. Jesus shook people to their core, because he freely embraced Isaiah's description of the Messiah as Suffering Servant—wounded, crushed, and bruised (Isaiah 53). "No one has greater love than this, to lay down one's life for one's friends" (John 15:13).

Strength in Prayer

A good Jew, Jesus faithfully kept Torah. Just as he had as a teen, Jesus lived in God's Presence and often encountered him, alone, in prayer. There he found renewed strength to fulfill his life's purpose, "to seek out and to save the lost" (Luke 19:10). With passion born of truth, he announced God's kingdom was here, "within you" (Luke 17:21), and offered salvation to all—sinners and saints, Jews and Gentiles.

But Jesus was uncompromising when he confronted any situation that wasn't right with God. He told his own people, people he knew were unfairly oppressed, that we are all sinners and need to repent (Luke 13:3). He accused the Pharisees of making life hard for people with their manmade rules (Matthew 23:4); some, like the prohibition against healing on the Sabbath, he questioned and broke (Mark 3:1–6). With a presence so powerful no one dared stop him, he defied the corrupt Sadducee priests who ruled the Temple.

Did Jesus learn this extraordinary courage from his parents? Years before, Joseph had ignored whispers that Mary cheated on him. He committed to and married the woman he loved—Jesus' mother, pregnant with him—rather than taking the "easy out" the Law offered. Mary always accepted God's will, whether it meant uprooting her family and moving to pagan Egypt or being ignored so her son could serve others. Did their example inspire Jesus and strengthen his willingness to do the same?

Darkness Gives Way to Glory

Jesus understood the consequences of publicly shaming those who considered themselves righteous—proud leaders, who felt they were above others and above the Law. In Jesus' culture, that demanded retaliation. But even as their plot to silence him gathered momentum, Jesus never backed down. He was the Lamb of God. His blood would seal a New Covenant in a kingdom that welcomed everyone.

Jesus had shown the world the Face of God. He taught us how to live. But when it was time, with calm purpose, he set in motion the events that led to his death, a death the angel foretold to Joseph: "She will bear a son, and you are to name him Jesus, for he will save his people from their sins" (Matthew 1:21).

Jesus didn't explain in the Gospels why good people suffer and die. But when he faced the darkest evil himself, he surrendered to God—though he couldn't feel God near. He urged his followers not to be afraid of what was coming, but to trust the reality of God's love. "The hairs of your head are all counted" (Matthew 10:30).

As his enemies closed in, Jesus predicted final victory. "Take courage; I have conquered the world!" (John 16:33). He had lived by the words he spoke that final night: "I give you a new commandment,

A rolling stone used to seal tombs, such as the one where Jesus was laid (Mark 16:3). "He is not here, but has risen" (Luke 24:5).

Photo Credit: Todd Bolen/BiblePlaces.com

that you love one another. Just as I have loved you, you also should love one another" (John 13:34–35).

Love. That's what Jesus was all about. That's what drove what he did all day and why he laid down his life for us. He lives! *Alleluia!*

Questions for Discussion

1. Jesus often took a stand regarding his beliefs. Think about casting the moneychangers from the Temple. How have you handled a face-to-face confrontation with someone who strongly disagreed with you? How did you find enough common ground to resolve your issues? Or, if not, why not? Did you agree to disagree, so you could remain friends? Or did you lose a friend?

2. Because Jesus' story is so familiar, it's hard to imagine its impact on someone who's never before heard it. There is a story about a girl who lived in the Soviet Union when its atheistic government had banned religion and turned churches into museums. Somehow, she found a copy of Luke's Gospel. After meeting Jesus for the first time in its pages, the teen said she "fell in love with him." What do you think struck her most? Why? What Gospel story still moves you in a powerful way? How is it possible to fall in love with God?

Time Line²

2000 BC	Abraham makes a covenant with God.
1500–1400 BC	Moses renews the Chosen People's covenant.
950 BC	King Solomon builds the First Temple in Jerusalem.
587–586 BC	Babylonians destroy the First Temple and drive Jews into exile.
538 BC	Chosen People return to the Holy Land; construction of a Second Temple begins later.
332–329 BC	Alexander the Great conquers the Holy Land.
150–100 BC	Qumran originally settled.
63 BC	Roman General Pompey conquers Jerusalem.
37 BC	Romans make Herod the Great king of Judea; a master builder, he takes on his greatest project—rebuilding the Second Temple.
31 BC	Earthquake destroys Qumran settlement; Egyptians see the defeat and deaths of Antony and Cleopatra.
27 BC–14 AD	Emperor Augustus rules the Roman Empire, including the Holy Land; his reign includes Jesus' boyhood and teen years.
6–4 BC	Jesus is born.
4 BC	King Herod the Great dies. Soon after, the Jews revolt and the Romans destroy the rebel city of Sepphoris, near Nazareth. Herod's son, King Herod Antipas, begins his rule in Galilee and rebuilds Sepphoris into his capital.

2. Except for those that can be verified historically, most are approximate dates.

6 AD	The Zealots, under Judas of Galilee, rise in revolt.
14–37 AD	Emperor Tiberius rules the Roman Empire; his reign includes Jesus' young adulthood and adulthood.
18 AD	In Jerusalem, Caiaphas becomes the Temple's High Priest.
27 AD	Pontius Pilate becomes the fifth prefect of Judea. Jesus begins his public ministry around this time.
28 AD	King Herod Antipas kills Jesus' cousin, John the Baptist.
30 AD	Jesus is crucified and rises from the dead.
37 AD	Josephus, the Jewish historian, is born.
48 AD	Council of Jerusalem (Church's first meeting; accepts Gentiles).
50s–60s AD	St. Paul writes his Letters, called Epistles.
65–95 AD	The Four Gospels (Matthew, Mark, Luke, and John) preserved in written form and in the Greek language.
66 AD	First Great Jewish Revolt against the Roman Empire begins. Josephus witnesses and records the story.
70 AD	Jerusalem falls to the Roman General Titus, who destroys the Second Temple and ends the First Revolt. A band of Zealots heads for Masada, Herod's fortified palace atop a plateau in the Judean Desert, to make their last stand.
73 AD	Roman soldiers finally overrun Masada, the last Jewish holdout. Inside, they find all the rebels had committed suicide, rather than be taken alive.
132–135 AD	The Second Great Jewish Revolt, commanded by Simon Bar-Kokhba and crushed by the Roman Emperor Hadrian.

Glossary

Adonai/Elohim/Shaddai/Ha-Shem: Hebrew names for God, used instead of the unspoken *Yahweh*; each had a slightly different meaning.

Alleluia: from the Hebrew words for "Praise God!"

Amen: a Hebrew word that signifies confirmation at the end of a prayer. It's usually translated "Truly," "May this come to pass," or "So be it!"

Amidah: central prayer of the Jewish synagogue, it contains praise, requests, and thanksgiving. Recited while standing, it was called the Eighteen Blessings in Jesus' time.

Antonia Fortress: Roman soldiers' barracks that adjoined the Second Temple along one high wall, allowing the pagan soldiers to peer down on Jews gathered for worship.

blessings: gifts God gives to us, and the praise, thanks, and gifts we give back to God.

cistern: a manmade holding area, dug into the ground and plastered over, used for collecting and storing water.

Court of the Gentiles: outermost Court of the Temple, where people gathered to hear rabbis preach under massive shaded porches. Gentiles could go no further.

Dead Sea: the world's saltiest body of water, located in the Holy Land's Jordan Valley.

Essenes: a movement likely begun by the house of Zadok (son of Aaron and high priest in Solomon's time) that opposed Hasmonean king/priests and strictly followed the Law.

First Great Revolt: begun by Jews against the Romans in 66 AD. It ended in 70 AD with the destruction of Jerusalem, though some Zealots held out at Masada until 73 AD.

First Temple: built by King Solomon with grandeur and described in 1 Kings 6.

fringes: tassels on a Jewish man's cloak, or *tallit*.

Galilee: Holy Land's northern region that includes the village of Nazareth. As a rabbi, Jesus frequently taught in towns and villages that surrounded the Sea of Galilee.

Gentiles: non-Jews; the Chosen People considered them pagan outsiders and avoided contact with them.

Hanukkah (Lights): the Jewish winter holiday. Today, families celebrate the rededication of the Temple (after the victorious Maccabean Revolt) by lighting a *menorah*, eating traditional foods fried in oil (like potato pancakes and jelly doughnuts), playing with *dreidels* (four-sided spinning tops), and giving gifts.

Hasmonean Dynasty: Jewish royal family; descendants of the warrior Maccabees after they defeated the Syrian ruler Antiochus and rededicated the Temple he had desecrated. During the Hasmonean rule (141–37 BC), each king acted as high priest.

Herod Antipas: son of Herod the Great and ruler of Galilee in Jesus' time.

Herod the Great: master builder, shrewd politician, and Rome's appointed king of the Jewish people. (Rome had added the Holy Land to its territory in 63 BC.) His reign (37–4 BC) included Jesus' birth, around 6 BC.

Herodians: favored, wealthy Jewish landowners in King Herod's time.

Holy of Holies: the Temple's highest and innermost sanctuary and most sacred space. Gold-plated and veiled, it was located within the towering building called the House of God, which stood at one end of the Priests' Court. Empty by Jesus' time, the Holy of Holies had once held the lost Ark of the Covenant.

Jordan River: where John the Baptist baptized Jesus and recognized him as the Messiah.

Josephus: a first-century Jewish historian, whose writings include his own eyewitness account of Jerusalem's final days.

Judea: Roman name for the conquered territory of the Holy Land; its people were known as "Judeans." Judea is also the name of the country's southern region, the old kingdom of Judah, which includes the city of Jerusalem and the town of Bethlehem.

kashrut: Jewish dietary laws that tell observant Jews which foods are "clean" (*kosher* or "fit" to eat) and which foods are "unclean" (to be avoided).

Levites: descendants of Levi, one of Jacob's twelve sons; Moses and his brother Aaron belonged to Levi's tribe. Aaron, his sons, and their descendants were chosen to be the priestly class; one officiated as high priest. Levites, other men from the tribe, took turns as Temple helpers, assisting priests with sacrificial duties and worship music.

Maccabees: Jewish warrior family who, under Judah/Judas Maccabee, won freedom from Greek and Syrian oppression around 164 BC. Some twenty years later, Simon Maccabaeus founded the Hasmonean Dynasty (141–37 BC). Queen Salome Alexandra ruled the dynasty from 76–67 BC and is mentioned in the Dead Sea Scrolls. Her two sons, Aristobul and Hyrcanus, began the fight that Rome came to the Holy Land to settle.

Men's Court/Court of Israel: where Jewish men stood to participate in Temple worship. Massive gates and wide stairways separated it from the lower-level Women's Court and the higher-level Priests' Court.

menorah: seven-branched golden candlestick that symbolized God's Presence in the Temple.

Messiah: Hebrew for "anointed;" the word is translated *Christos* in Greek and *Christus* in Latin. According to the Torah, the Chosen People anointed with oil their kings (1 Samuel 10:1), priests (Exodus 29:29), and prophets (Isaiah 61:1). Thus, "Messiah/the Anointed One" had a sacred and powerful meaning.

mezuzah: tiny rolled scroll, inscribed with part of the *Shema*, and placed inside a decorated case. The case hangs, slanted, on the doorpost of Jewish homes (sometimes on inside doorways, too). It's customary to kiss or touch it when entering or leaving.

midrash: Hebrew for "search" or "seek;" the word refers to the rabbis' thoughtful exploration of Scripture to interpret the meanings of passages for the Chosen People.

midrash haggadah: ancient collection of Jewish storytelling (parables, legends, and homilies) used by rabbis to help the people better understand Scripture. This nonlegal *midrash* was oral in Jesus' day.

midrash halakah: Jewish religious law; Scripture-based rules and teachings that applied Moses' Law to everyday Jewish life. This legal *midrash*, also oral, was meant to encourage God's people to live rightly.

mikveh: a stepped, plastered pool or bath that "gathered" or collected water directly from natural sources. A *mikveh* had to hold at least 200 gallons. Jews descended into this water until they were totally immersed, thus becoming cleansed or ritually pure.

Mishna ("repetition"): Oral Torah; the rabbis' multiple rulings on Scripture, as well as wise sayings. Oral Torah was unwritten in Jesus' time.

mitzvot (plural of *mitzvah*): good deeds and acts of kindness, which Jews are obliged or commanded to perform.

Nazareth: small Galilean "village of the branch" of King David, where Jesus grew up.

Nazarites: men and women who vowed to live apart from the community for a time. They did not drink wine, cut their hair, or touch the dead during their time of consecration. Because of his desert lifestyle, some scholars wonder if John the Baptist had ever taken the Nazarite vow.

Nazoreans: members of a Jewish clan/family who "sprouted" like a "branch" (*nezer*) from King David's royal line. Some scholars think this Davidic clan settled in and around Nazareth, and that Jesus belonged to it—which might explain why Matthew refers to him being called a Nazorean (Matthew 2:23).

New Covenant: the reign of God's kingdom over all people. Based on selfless love for God and neighbor, this agreement was sealed with Jesus' blood on Calvary.

Old Covenant: the Chosen People's age-old agreement with God. Based on fear of (and punishment for) breaking the Ten Commandments and Moses' Law, it was made on Mount Sinai and sealed with the blood of sacrificial animals.

ossuary: a stone bone box or burial box, in which a dead person's bones were placed after a year in the family's burial cave.

Passover: spring Jewish holiday that commemorates God saving the Chosen People from the tenth plague, when the Lord killed every firstborn in Egypt, but "passed over" Jewish homes that had lamb's blood smeared on the doorposts (Exodus 12:1–32). Pharaoh finally allowed the people to "pass over" into freedom.

Pentecost: the Jewish spring festival of Weeks or First Fruits (*Shavuot*), when the finest wheat was offered in the Temple around fifty days after Passover. This feast coincided with the end of the grain harvest, since wheat was the last cereal crop to ripen.

Pharisees (rabbis): lay scholars and teachers of Moses' Law, who believed in *both* Written and Oral Torah (unlike their adversaries, the Temple priests or Sadducees).

phylacteries (*tefillin*): small, black leather boxes that contain tiny Scripture scrolls; a Jewish man straps them on his forehead and one arm.

Pool of Siloam: Jerusalem water source, fed by the Gihon Spring; where Jesus cured the blind man (John 9:6–7).

priests: refers to the Sadducees, descendants of Aaron and opponents of the Pharisees, who were chosen by the Sanhedrin to offer sacrifice and conduct the Temple liturgy.

Priests' Court: Temple's holy place of sacrifice, elevated above the three lower Courts. Its "House of God" enclosed the Holy of Holies and held sacred furniture used in worship (examples include the gold incense altar and the golden *menorah*).

Purim (Lots): spring festival that commemorates how Queen Esther saved her people from a death plot by revealing to her Persian husband that she, too, was Jewish.

rabbi: Hebrew for "my master." In Jesus' day, it was used as a respectful form of address for a wise teacher (sage/Pharisee) or someone in authority.

ritual bath: see *mikveh*.

ritual purity: the Mishna's seder that discusses one's spiritual contamination by anything the Bible calls "unclean," including human and animal corpses, blood, pus, and lepers; this seder also discusses ritual actions for purification.

Rosh Hoshana (Trumpets): autumn festival that is the Jewish New Year.

Sabbath: see *Shabbat*.

Sadducees: class of aristocratic priests and descendants of the Hasmonean king/high priests, who conducted the Temple liturgy. Wealthy opponents of the Pharisees and Essenes, they adopted Hellenism (Greek thinking) and believed only in Written Torah.

Samaria: middle region of the Holy Land in Jesus' day. Samaritans claimed Jewish heritage, but worshipped *Yahweh* on Mount Gerizim. Hostility existed between them and Jews who worshipped in Jerusalem's Temple. Most Jews considered Samaritans a people of mixed blood and mixed religions, and detested them.

Sanhedrin: the highest judicial authority of the Jewish people, comparable to our Supreme Court. It was composed of a council of seventy-one members (both Pharisees and Sadducees) who met daily in the Temple.

scribes: Torah scholars and experts in the Law, who hand-copied Scripture and other important writings.

Sea of Galilee: a large, inland freshwater lake in the Holy Land's northern region. In Jesus' time, it was surrounded by villages and towns where fishing and trade thrived.

Second Great Revolt: begun in 132 AD, it was commanded by Simon Bar-Kokhba and crushed by the Roman Emperor Hadrian in 135 AD.

Second Temple: Herod the Great's reconstruction of Solomon's First Temple. King Herod Antipas continued his father's project into Jesus' adult years and beyond.

Second Temple Period: (100 BC–100 AD) roughly the time from the first century BC (Before Christ) to the first century AD (*Anno Domini*, Latin for "Year of the Lord," which marks the years after Jesus' birth, or After Christ). Today, some people use BCE (Before the Common Era) instead of BC and CE (Common Era) for AD.

Seder: Hebrew word for "order" and the name for the Passover meal, which today includes reading the Exodus story, singing songs, praising God, drinking wine, and eating prescribed foods—all in a specific order.

seders: the comprehensive six orders of the Mishna, thought to be based on Oral Torah and later recorded by rabbis in written form.

Seders include: Seeds (Food) and Blessings, Sabbath and Festivals, Women, Damages, Temple Rituals, and Ritual Purity.

Sepphoris: city located near the village of Nazareth in Galilee. Once a stronghold of Jewish rebels, it was destroyed by the Romans and rebuilt by Herod Antipas.

Shabbat (Sabbath): Saturday, the seventh day of the Jewish week, set apart for prayer, Scripture study, and rest.

Shavuot: see Pentecost.

shekel (Hebrew for "weight"): a silver coin used in the Holy Land in Jesus' day; its exact weight is still not known.

Shekinah: Hebrew word that signifies the Divine Presence of God.

Shema: Jewish declaration of faith, a powerful prayer recited every morning and evening. The opening line, *"Hear, O Israel, the Lord is our God, the Lord alone,"* is taken from Written Torah (Deuteronomy 6:4–9).

Sukkoth (Tabernacles/Booths)—autumn holiday when families rejoiced over the grape and olive harvests and lived outdoors for a week in "tabernacles" (tents) or "booths" (huts made of branches) to remember their ancestors' 40 years of wandering in the desert.

synagogue: in Jesus' day, an assembly hall for the Jewish community, an elementary school for its young boys, and a house of prayer and study for its adult men and women. Synagogues became vital as Jewish houses of worship after the Romans destroyed the Temple in Jerusalem in 70 A.D, ending animal sacrifices and scattering the priests.

tallit: Hebrew for the long fringed cloak or mantle worn by Jewish men in Jesus' time. Today it refers to a short prayer shawl.

Talmud: the rabbis' extensive commentary on the Mishna, including religious laws written down after Jesus' day.

tefillin (phylacteries): small, black leather boxes that contain tiny Scripture scrolls; a Jewish man straps them on his forehead and one arm.

tekhelet: Hebrew word for a beautiful and expensive blue dye, obtained from sea snails.

tekton: Greek word for "artisan" or "skilled workman," used in the Bible to describe the profession of Joseph and Jesus; it can mean a carpenter, metal smith, or stone mason.

Torah: traditional Jewish Law, both Written and Oral in form. Written Torah is comprised of the first five books of Hebrew Scripture (Genesis, Exodus, Leviticus, Numbers, and Deuteronomy). The Law of Moses, it is believed to have been dictated by God. Oral Torah (contained in the Mishna/Talmud) is the rabbis' long commentary on Written Torah, and is used for study. The Mishna is divided into six orders; each order is divided into tractates: each tractate is divided into chapters, and each chapter has a number of *halakah*, or religious laws.

tractates: Mishna/Talmud's total of sixty-three books, long expositions on the seders.

tunic: basic first-century, hand-woven garment—a wide-sleeved and belted linen robe that reached just below a man's knees and to a woman's ankles.

Women's Court: where Jewish women observed and prayed in the Temple. It had a balcony, benches for public assembly, and boxes for donations.

Yahweh: The Hebrews' unspeakable Name of God, "I am Who I am," written *YHWH*.

Yom Kippur (Day of Atonement): holiest day of the year, when Jews observe the "great fast" and, in Jesus' time, a scapegoat bearing their sins was driven into the desert.

Zealots: a Messiah-centered, extremist Jewish sect that began in Galilee around 6 AD. Zealots rioted constantly against Roman rule.

Selected Bibliography and Author/Source Credentials

Bailey, Kenneth E.—Emeritus Research Professor of Middle Eastern New Testament Studies for Jerusalem's Tantur Ecumenical Institute.
  Jesus Through Middle Eastern Eyes: Cultural Studies in the Gospels. Downers Grove, IL: IVP Academic, 2008.

Bauckham, Richard—Professor of New Testament Studies, University of St. Andrews, Scotland.
  Jesus and the Eyewitnesses. Grand Rapids, MI: William B. Eerdmans, 2006.

Bivin, David—Codirector with his wife, Josa, of *Jerusalem Perspective* and founding member of the Jerusalem School of Synoptic Research.
  New Light on the Difficult Words of Jesus. Holland, MI: En-Gedi Resource Center, 2005.

Blech, Rabbi Benjamin—Associate Professor of Talmud at Yeshiva University in New York.
  The Complete Idiot's Guide to Understanding Judaism. Indianapolis: Alpha Books, 1999.

Bolen, Todd—Holy Land photographer and Associate Professor of Biblical Studies at The Master's College.

Borowski, Oded—Associate Professor of Biblical Archaeology and Hebrew at Emory University.
  Daily Life in Biblical Times. Atlanta, GA: Society of Biblical Literature, 2003.

Buddemeyer-Porter, Mary—Author, educator, and Christian lecturer.
  Will I See Fido in Heaven? Manchester, MO: Eden Publications, 2006.

Burge, Gary M.—Professor of New Testament at Wheaton College; expert in the ancient Jewish background of the Bible.

The Bible and the Land. Ancient Context Ancient Faith Series. Grand Rapids, MI: Zondervan, 2009.

_____. *Encounters with Jesus.* Grand Rapids, MI: Zondervan, 2010.

_____. *Jesus, the Middle Eastern Storyteller.* Grand Rapids, MI: Zondervan, 2009.

Charlesworth, James H.—Professor of New Testament Language and Literature; Director of the Dead Sea Scrolls Project at Princeton Theological Seminary.

The Historical Jesus: An Essential Guide. Nashville, TN: Abingdon Press, 2008.

_____, ed. *Jesus and Archaeology.* Grand Rapids, MI: William B. Eerdmans, 2006.

Cross, Frank Moore Jr. (1921–2012)—Professor at Harvard University and Dead Sea Scrolls' translator.

Daniel-Rops, Henri (1901–1965)—French historian and Holy Land scholar.

Daily Life in Palestine at the Time of Christ. London: Phoenix Press, English trans. 1962, paperback ed. 2002.

The Dead Sea Scrolls. Washington, DC: Biblical Archaeology Society and Society of Biblical Literature, 2007.

Eshel, Hanan (1958–2010)—Professor of Archaeology at Bar-Ilan University, Israel.

Evans, Craig A.—Payzant Distinguished Professor of New Testament at Acadia Divinity College in Nova Scotia; editor, consultant, and author of many books on the New Testament.

Jesus and His World: The Archaeological Evidence. Louisville, KY: Westminster John Knox Press, 2012.

_____, and N. T. Wright—Bishop of Durham in the Church of England. Edited by Troy A. Miller. *Jesus, the Final Days: What Really Happened.* Louisville, KY: Westminster John Knox Press, 2009.

Flusser, David (1917–2000)—Professor of Early Christianity and Judaism of the Second Temple Period at the Hebrew University of Jerusalem; highly honored and prolific author.

  With R. Steven Notley. *The Sage from Galilee: Rediscovering Jesus' Genius.* Grand Rapids, MI: William B. Eerdmans, 2007.

Hezser, Catherine—Professor of Jewish Studies at the School of Oriental and African Studies, University of London.

  The Oxford Handbook of Jewish Daily Life in Roman Palestine. New York: Oxford University Press, 2010.

King, Philip J., Rev.—Professor Emeritus of Biblical Studies at Boston University—and Lawrence E. Stager—Dorot Professor of the Archaeology of Israel at Harvard University.

  Life in Biblical Israel. Louisville, KY: Westminster John Knox Press, 2001.

Kloner, Amos—Archaeologist and Associate Professor, Department of the Land of Israel Studies at Bar-Ilan University.

Magness, Jodi—Kenan Distinguished Professor for Teaching Excellence in Early Judaism, University of North Carolina at Chapel Hill; lecturer and author.

  Stone and Dung, Oil and Spit: Jewish Daily Life in the Time of Jesus. Grand Rapids, MI: William B. Eerdmans, 2011.

Maier, Paul L.—Professor of Ancient History at Western Michigan University.

  Trans. and ed. *Josephus: The Essential Writings.* Grand Rapids, MI: Kregel Publications, 1988.

Malina, Bruce J.—Professor, Department of Theology, Creighton University.

  The New Testament World: Insights from Cultural Anthropology. Louisville, KY: Westminster John Knox Press, 2001.

Mason, Steve—Professor of Humanities at Vanier College, York University, Ontario.

Josephus and the New Testament. Peabody, MA: Hendrickson Publishers, 2003.

McKenzie, John L., SJ (1910–1991)—Professor at DePaul University, Chicago.

Dictionary of the Bible. New York: Simon & Schuster, 1965; Macmillan, 1995.

McNamer, Elizabeth—Assistant Professor at Rocky Mountain College, Billings, Montana; director of the Bethsaida Excavation Project, Israel—and Bargil Pixner (see page 129).

Jesus and First-Century Christianity in Jerusalem. New York/Mahwah, NJ: Paulist Press, 2008.

Meyers, Eric M.—Professor of Judaic Studies at Duke University; archaeologist, author.

Morse, Kitty—Moroccan-born author of books on Mediterranean cooking.

A Biblical Feast: Foods from the Holy Land. Berkeley, CA: Ten Speed Press, 1998.

Moseley, Dr. Ron—Pastor; founder of the Arkansas Institute of Holy Land Studies.

Yeshua: A Guide to the Real Jesus and the Original Church. Baltimore, MD: Lederer Books, 1996.

Murphy-O'Connor, Jerome, OP—Dominican Professor of the New Testament at the Ecole Biblique et Archeologique Francaise in Jerusalem.

The Holy Land: An Archaeological Guide from the Earliest Times to 1700. New York: Oxford University Press, 1986 (revised).

Notley, R. Steven—Distinguished Professor of New Testament and Christian Origins (Nyack College, New York City campus) and member of the Jerusalem School of Synoptic Research—and Ze'ev Safrai—Professor of Land of Israel Studies at Bar-Ilan University, Israel.

Parables of the Sages: Jewish Wisdom from Jesus to Rav Ashi. Jerusalem: Carta, 2011.

Parry, Rabbi Aaron—Jewish religious leader and educator; lived seven years in Israel.

The Complete Idiot's Guide to the Talmud. New York: Alpha Books, 2004.

Pilch, John J.—Professor of Scripture at Georgetown University.

The Cultural Dictionary of the Bible. Collegeville, MN: Liturgical Press, 1999.

_____. *Cultural Tools for Interpreting the Good News.* Collegeville, MN: Liturgical Press, 2002.

_____. *The Cultural World of Jesus: Sunday by Sunday, Cycle A.* Collegeville, MN: Liturgical Press, 1995.

_____. *The Cultural World of Jesus: Sunday by Sunday, Cycle B.* Collegeville, MN: Liturgical Press, 1996.

_____. *The Cultural World of Jesus: Sunday by Sunday, Cycle C.* Collegeville, MN: Liturgical Press, 1997.

Pixner, Bargil, OSB (1921–2002)—Benedictine monk; pursued Jewish-Christian studies and archaeological research from Dormition Abbey on Mount Zion and the Monastery of Tabgha.

Paths of the Messiah and Sites of the Early Church from Galilee to Jerusalem: Jesus and Jewish Christianity in Light of Archaeological Discoveries. Edited by Rainer Riesner. San Francisco, CA: Ignatius Press, 2010 (Original German edition, 1991).

_____. *With Jesus through Galilee: According to the Fifth Gospel.* Rosh Pina, Israel: Corazin Publishing, 1992.

_____. *With Jesus in Jerusalem: His First and Last Days in Judea.* Rosh Pina, Israel: Corazin Publishing, 1996.

Punton, Anne—Author and lecturer on the Jewish roots of Christianity; spent twelve years in Israel.

The World Jesus Knew. Grand Rapids, MI: Monarch Books, 1996.

Reed, Jonathan L.—Professor of New Testament and Christian Origins at the University of LaVerne, California; field director of the Sepphoris Acropolis Excavations.

Archaeology and the Galilean Jesus: A Re-Examination of the Evidence. Harrisburg, PA: Trinity Press International, 2000.

Reich, Ronny—Professor of Archaeology at the University of Haifa, Israel.

Excavating the City of David: Where Jerusalem's History Began. Jerusalem: Israel Exploration Society and Biblical Archaeology Society, 2011.

Ritmeyer, Leen & Kathleen—Husband (archaeological architect) and wife (archaeologist) team at Temple Mount excavations.

Secrets of Jerusalem's Temple Mount. Washington, DC: Biblical Archaeology Society, 2006.

Safrai, Baruch—Longtime excavator of his native Israel's archaeological sites.

Safrai, Shmuel (1919–2003)—Esteemed rabbi, author, and Professor Emeritus of Jewish History of the Mishnaic and Talmudic Period at the Hebrew University of Jerusalem. Many of his writings can be found at the Jerusalem Perspective website.

Shanks, Hershel—Founder and editor of *Biblical Archaeology Review* magazine; author and editor of many Biblical Archaeology Society publications.

Ed. *Ancient Israel: From Abraham to the Roman Destruction of the Temple.* 3rd ed. Upper Saddle River, NJ: Prentice Hall and Washington, DC: Biblical Archaeology Society, 2011.

_____ , ed. *Christianity and Rabbinic Judaism: A Parallel History of Their Origins and Early Development.* Washington, DC: Biblical Archaeology Society, 1992.

_____. *The Copper Scroll and the Search for the Temple Treasure.* Washington, DC: Biblical Archaeology Society, 2007.

_____. *The Dead Sea Scrolls: Discovery and Meaning* (e-book). Washington, DC: Biblical Archaeology Society, 2007.

_____, ed. *Where Christianity Was Born: A Collection from the Biblical Archaeology Society.* Washington, DC: Biblical Archaeology Society, 2006.

Spangler, Ann—Award-winning spiritual writer—and Dr. Lois Tverberg—Author, speaker, and cofounder of the En-Gedi Resource Center.

Sitting at the Feet of Rabbi Jesus: How the Jewishness of Jesus Can Transform Your Faith. Grand Rapids, MI: Zondervan, 2009.

Strange, James F.—Professor of Religious Studies at the University of South Florida; directed excavations at Sepphoris since 1983.

Strobel, Lee—Pastor and former award-winning journalist at the *Chicago Tribune.*

The Case for Christ: A Journalist's Personal Investigation of the Evidence for Jesus. Grand Rapids, MI: Zondervan Publishing House, 1998.

Tzaferis, Vassilios—Archaeologist and former Director of Excavations and Surveys for the Israel Antiquities Authority; discovered heel bone of crucifixion victim.

Vamosh, Miriam Feinberg—Holy Land researcher and author.

Daily Life at the Time of Jesus. Nashville, TN: AbingdonPress, 2001.

_____. *Food at the Time of the Bible: From Adam's Apple to the Last Supper.* Nashville, TN: Abingdon Press, 2004.

VanderKam, James C.—Professor of Theology at the University of Notre Dame; language expert and editor of the Dead Sea Scrolls.

Vos, Howard F.—Emeritus Professor of History and Archaeology at The King's College in Tuxedo, New York.

Nelson's New Illustrated Bible Manners and Customs: How the People of the Bible Really Lived. Nashville, TN: Thomas Nelson Publishers, 1999.

Wachsmann, Shelley—Professor of Biblical Archaeology at Texas A&M University; specialist in Underwater Archaeology.

Young, Brad H.—PhD from Hebrew University; president and founder of the Gospel Research Foundation.

Jesus, the Jewish Theologian. Peabody, MA: Hendrickson Publishers, 1995.

_____. *The Parables: Jewish Traditions and Christian Interpretation.* Peabody, MA: Hendrickson Publishers, 1998.